T0328740

THE GENERAL EYRE

THE GENERAL EYRE

LECTURES DELIVERED IN THE UNIVERSITY
OF LONDON AT THE REQUEST OF
THE FACULTY OF LAWS

BY

WILLIAM CRADDOCK BOLLAND, M.A.

*Of Lincoln's Inn, Barrister-at-Law; late Scholar
of Magdalene College, Cambridge*

WITH AN INTRODUCTION

BY

HAROLD DEXTER HAZELTINE, M.A., Litt.D.

*Of the Inner Temple, Barrister-at-Law; Downing Professor of the
Laws of England in the University of Cambridge*

CAMBRIDGE
AT THE UNIVERSITY PRESS
1922

CAMBRIDGE
UNIVERSITY PRESS

University Printing House, Cambridge CB2 8BS, United Kingdom

Cambridge University Press is part of the University of Cambridge.

It furthers the University's mission by disseminating knowledge in the pursuit of education, learning and research at the highest international levels of excellence.

www.cambridge.org
Information on this title: www.cambridge.org/9781107536944

First published 1922
First paperback edition 2015

A catalogue record for this publication is available from the British Library

ISBN 978-1-107-53694-4 Paperback

PREFACE

THIS course of lectures on the General Eyre follows on very naturally after the previous course on the Year Books, for the Year Books form the chief source of what we know about the eyres. It is in them alone that we can see the eyres actually alive and at work. The old legal writers, Bracton and the rest, have, indeed, coldly pictured for us something of their form and told us something of their functions, but it was left to the writers of the Year Books to breathe the living spirit into this lifeless form. And here, not only for myself but also for those from whom I have learned almost all I know about the eyres, the writers of these manuscripts of long ago, I would thank the University of London for the opportunity it gave me in these lectures of recovering from the oblivion of centuries and bringing back to light all the lore of the eyres which these ancients wrote down for the instruction of the lawyers and law-students of their own day, and which is of great value now to students of many other branches of learning.

If I should seem in these lectures to have over-stressed somewhat the financial side of the eyres and under-stated their judicial side, it must be remembered that I had only a narrowly limited time wherein to deal with a very wide subject. It was necessary, therefore, to insist more upon those matters which were especially characteristic of the eyres than upon those which were not. On their purely judicial side in the trial of pleas of one sort and another, they differed not at all, as I have stated in the lectures, from a session of the Court of Common Bench at Westminster. Hence arises what may, perhaps, appear an over-weighting of the financial scale of the balance as against the judicial one. In the circumstances I am afraid that this was scarcely avoidable.

My thanks are due and very sincerely given to Professor Hazeltine for his kindly and illuminating Introduction to this volume. It contains more than one valuable suggestion which I hope that I or another may have an opportunity of carrying out. In the meantime I am very glad to have them.

W. C. B.

December, 1921.

CONTENTS

INTRODUCTION

THE importance of the administrative work of the king's justices in eyre during more than two centuries of the middle age has long been recognised. Until they decayed and perished in the fourteenth century, superseded by the justices of assize and other rival commissions, the eyre courts were powerful instruments of royal authority in the shires; and yet our standard legal histories contain but brief and incomplete accounts of their activities. The chief reason for this neglect lies in the fact that the greater part of our information is still embodied in a mass of unprinted manuscript materials, principally plea rolls and year books. Printed editions of the medieval law writers—Glanvill, Bracton, Britton, and Fleta—tell us indeed something about the powers and work of the eyres; something also we learn from Hoveden's *Chronicle* and from the *Liber Custumorum* and *Liber Albus* of the City of London. Plea rolls of two or three of the eyres of Edward I are included in the series of year books edited by Horwood; extracts from eyre rolls of Henry III's justices are to be found in Maitland's edition of Bracton's *Note Book*; and in his *Pleas of the Crown for the County of Gloucester* Maitland has transcribed portions of the record of the eyre of 1221 in that shire. But what of the year books of the eyres, the reports of cases which supplement and illumine in so many fruitful ways the bare record of the plea rolls? Has any scholar made accessible in printed form even a small part of that vast treasure of manuscripts?

The answer to this question—an answer already familiar to medievalists—introduces at once the name of my learned friend Mr Bolland, who has invited me to write a few paragraphs by way of introduction to this volume of lectures. Mr Bolland is the one scholar who by his extended researches among the manuscript year books of the eyres has made himself the master of their contents; and certain of the results of his studies he has embodied in three volumes on *The Eyre of Kent: 6 and 7 Edward II* (1313–14), and in a volume of *Select Bills in Eyre* (1292–1333), all recently published by the Selden Society. In these volumes we possess not only an accurate transcript of the texts, but also the editor's notes and his valuable introductory essays on the history of the eyres.

Mr Bolland, therefore, came to his task as a lecturer on the general eyre with a knowledge unequalled by any other scholar of our time; and by publishing his lectures in their present form he has communicated his learning to a still wider audience. We have here presented to us in *The General Eyre* a living picture of the actual working of the institution during the period of its ascendency; while the historical background for this picture—the background of communal, municipal, seignorial, royal, and ecclesiastical courts—is also sketched in clear outline. We behold the king's justices of the general eyre journeying to every shire of the realm under the most comprehensive of all judicial commissions, the commission to entertain all manner of pleas, the commission *ad omnia placita,* civil and criminal; and we behold also the sheriffs, the coroners, the many dozens of jurymen, the prisoners, the parties to civil proceedings, as they appear before the representatives of kingly power. The whole life of the shire centres for the time being in the court of the king's itinerant justices: and it is this life of which we may read in Mr Bolland's entertaining lectures.

The powers possessed by the justices of the general

eyre under their commission were royal powers, and royal powers so extensive that the justices invested with them represented the king in a way which made them, in Mr Bolland's words, almost "kings themselves within the county wherein they were in session." It was the possession of powers so vast that enabled the justices to hold pleas of the crown, to hear and determine assizes and actions of all kinds, to hold gaol deliveries, to try writs of *quo warranto*, to exercise not only a jurisdiction at law by writ process, but also a jurisdiction in equity under the informal procedure by bills in eyre. In dealing with the several aspects of this extensive jurisdiction Mr Bolland has drawn largely upon unpublished manuscript materials, especially the manuscript year books of eyres held during the reigns of the first three Edwards; and it is this reliance upon manuscript sources which gives the lectures a special place and value in our historical literature. To the history of several topics of the law, such as sanctuary, the deodand, the proof of Englishry and the fine, known as *murdrum*, inflicted in absence of this proof, Mr Bolland makes an original contribution; and he likewise throws fresh light on features of institutional history, such as the jury and the relation of itinerant justices to the local and central courts of the realm.

Of special interest is Mr Bolland's view that the justices of the general eyre were concerned but little with the administration of justice, their primary and all-absorbing task being the getting of money into the king's exchequer through the infliction of fines and amercements and in other ways. The justices were "out on a great money-making expedition for the king's benefit; the crown pleas division of the eyre was in fact, whatever it might be in theory, a travelling branch of the exchequer." No doubt Mr Bolland is right in his general conclusion; but it is possible that he has somewhat over-stressed the fiscal side of the eyre's business. In the age of which he writes revenue and justice were inextricably commingled. In certain of its aspects royal criminal justice was a harsh and terrible justice; and it was particularly this side of the eyre's work which made the coming of the justices a matter of dread to the whole county. Harsh and terrible though it was in many ways, it was nevertheless the justice of the time; and its traditions lingered long in the law of the land. Justice, we can hardly doubt, was in fact one of the main functions of the eyre; but fortunately for the king, and of this he was fully conscious, it was a justice which netted the exchequer a handsome return. When we turn from the criminal to the civil side of the eyre's jurisdiction, and particularly to the equitable procedure by bill in eyre, royal justice displayed a milder temper: here at least, so it would seem, justice predominated, over-riding the claims of revenue.

Mr Bolland has touched but lightly on the institutional relationship between the general eyre and the exchequer; and it may be hoped that at a future time he will explore this feature of constitutional growth more fully. From an early time justices in eyre seem to have been closely connected with the exchequer. In 1168, as Mr Bolland reminds us, a deputation of four barons of the exchequer journeyed through the country as itinerant justices and collectors of revenue. We know, in other ways, that many of the justices in eyre were men who sat at the exchequer board. Richard the Treasurer in his *Dialogus de Scaccario* tells us of the duties of the itinerant justices to the exchequer in the matter of their rolls. These are but a few of many scattered points which suggest a fruitful line of research.

Mr Bolland has very properly restricted his discourse to the history of the English eyres: he has not told us of their forerunners in Continental legal history, nor has he sketched the process by which the English eyre-system spread to regions outside England. These aspects of the full story of the eyre are worthy of careful study. One of the results of such study would be the placing of the English eyre in its true perspective of European legal development; and this is a subject to which Mr Bolland himself ought to turn his attention. His studies would no doubt convince him that Henry I did not invent the system of itinerant justices. Traces of this system in Anglo-Saxon times may have been due, as Stubbs suggests, to Frankish influence; but of this one cannot be quite sure. The true path of Frankish influence would seem to lie through Normandy. The Frankish system of royal *missi*, a system of itinerant judicial commissioners, did not perish with the fall of the Carolingian empire; for in that corner of the empire which became Normandy Frankish legal traditions persisted and became the basis of government and law. In Normandy the *missi* survived as the duke's itinerant justices; and from the duchy the institution was transplanted to England in the time of the Norman kings. As early as the reign of William the Conqueror the king's *missi* presided in some of the local courts of England. In spirit and in direct line of historical growth, the itinerant judicial commissioners of the English kings, including their justices of the general eyre, are the descendants of the *missi* of the Frankish rulers. It is this feature of English institutional and legal history, a feature as striking in its way as the derivation of the English jury from the Frankish *inquisitio*, which teaches us afresh how much of our legal system has its origin in Frankish and Frankish-Norman institutions. As part of that gradual and vast process of the spread of English legal institutions, the *missi*, the justices in eyre, have a further history in regions outside England. King John began the practice of commissioning justices in eyre in Ireland. In Scottish legal history the "justice-ayres," courts which closely resemble the English eyres, long held a conspicuous place in royal administration. We meet with traces of them as early as the time of David I (1124–53), a period when Norman influence in Scotland was strong: and it may well be that they were a conscious adaptation of the Anglo-Norman eyres to Scottish needs and conditions. Some day the history of the extension of English institutions and law beyond English borders will be written in detail. We may be sure that part of it will deal with the eyres.

The visitations of the justices of the general eyre meant much to the people of the middle age. From the point of view of social and legal evolution, they also mean much to us of the present day. Looking back on the work of an institution which ceased to function nearly six hundred years ago we can now see that the general eyre played its own special rôle in the training of the English people for self-government and in the growth of their common law. An institution which thus serves as one of the historical bases of present-day life and law must have much more than a mere antiquarian interest to men of our own time; and in Mr Bolland's learned and lively lectures, happily now published in this volume, they will find matter for their enlightenment.

H. D. HAZELTINE.

THE GENERAL EYRE

Lecture I

I AM to speak to you in these lectures of the mediaeval
General Eyre. It is always well to begin at the beginning,
but it is not always easy to say where the beginning is.
Such a great engine of law, finance and justice, as the
General Eyre in its later developments undoubtedly became, penetrating into all the remotest crannies of the
country and sweeping its searchlight over the life and
actions of every section of society, official and private,
did not spring into existence in its full stature and per-
fected form at any particular moment. Let us spend a
few preliminary minutes in reminding ourselves how and
where law and justice were administered in England in
the days of our early kings, in the days of William I and
his immediate successors, long before the General Eyre
had been heard of, that General Eyre which, when it
came along, swept into its net every court and every
jurisdiction within the county in which it was in session;
and at the same time peremptorily extinguished the jurisdiction of the King's Justices of the Bench sitting at
Westminster to deal with any action or matter affecting
interests in the same county. The courts known to the
English law in those early days, leaving out for the
moment the King's Court, the *Curia Regis*, and the Courts
Christian, about which I will say something later, may
be loosely divided into three classes, which we may call

communal, municipal and seignorial courts. This must be taken as a rough classification only. The legal theory of the time had not attained to a really scientific and definite one. The communal courts included county courts and such of the courts of the hundreds as had not passed by royal grants into private hands. What we have called municipal courts were courts held in chartered cities and boroughs, exercising such powers as the Sovereign by his charter had conferred upon them. The seignorial courts were what we are accustomed to call now Courts Baron. I have given you a bare and arid list of names, unnecessary to those who have already some knowledge of these matters, quite unilluminating and useless to those who have not. And so I must not leave the matter there. I will try as best I can to give you some sort of an account of some of these courts that will help you to realize what they were like, to remember who the people were who went to them, and what was done at them; a story of them that will, perhaps, enable you to carry away with you some recollections that may be real and helpful to you.

The county court was, I think we may say, the most important in a popular sense of all our early English courts, as it is certainly one of our most ancient institutions. But the mediaeval county court was not in the least like the county court of to-day. It was the court where the ordinary man ordinarily sought justice. Unfortunately for our present purpose it kept no official record of its proceedings, except in respect of a few minor matters, and so any reconstruction of these proceedings is more difficult than it would be in the case of a court which had kept a full record. Still we can gather much about it from old authorities; quite enough to put together an intelligible account of it. It met once a month, usually,

I suppose, in the county town, in the shire-hall where there was one; but it did not always meet in the county town or in any town at all. In that thirteenth century law tract which we know as *Hengham Magna* the writer tells us that the court frequently met in the open air and in out-of-the-way places in the country[1]. The court was summoned by the Sheriff, who, you will remember, was a distinctly royal officer, appointed by the King and dismissible by him at a moment's notice; and he was strictly accountable to the royal exchequer for all moneys that came into his hands by reason of his office, and these were many. Besides summoning the court, the Sheriff was the presiding officer. It was he who held the court. Up to William I's time the Bishop had been joined with him, but William separated the ecclesiastical jurisdiction of the county court from its civil jurisdiction, and relegated the Bishop to a court of his own, known as Court Christian, there to deal exclusively with such matters as were assigned to the ecclesiastical jurisdiction. The Sheriff "held the pleas." That is the technical expression. He regulated the whole proceedings, though in some matters he was assisted and checked by elective officers, the coroners of the county. He issued all mandates that were necessary; but he did not make the judgments. We shall see in a moment or two who did. In theory all the freeholders of the county were bound to attend their county court, and incurred penalties if they did not attend it. They were called the suitors of the court [*sectatores*] and their service or attendance there was called suit. This theory that all the freeholders of the county must attend the court, must give their suit there, was a workable one in very early

---

[1] "Frequenter euenit quod comitatus tenentur in siluis et campestribus foris uillis et alibi." Cap. IV.

days, but as the land became more and more divided into smaller parcels, and these again subdivided into still smaller ones, and each parcel of land carried an estate of freehold, the number of freeholders became too large for it to continue practically possible to insist upon the attendance of all of them at the court. Responsibility to do suit, to attend the county court, seems in process of time to have become attached to particular parcels of land. The final definite amount of suit to which the court had been entitled from some larger extent of land was apportioned out amongst those into whose hands smaller parcels, carved thereout, had come by purchase; and the men who were actually bound to attend the court were only those freeholders who were so bound by some sort of bargain, which was doubtless considered in the price paid for the land, which they or their predecessors in title had made when purchasing the land. It is these suitors of the court, those freeholders actually attending the court, who give the judgments when the time for a judgment comes.

The county court was for the most part a civil, non-criminal court, but it could entertain some of the initial proceedings in criminal cases. It had a full original jurisdiction in personal actions. Real actions, actions about interests in land, came to it when the feudal courts of the lords of manors made default in justice; and we hear of cases being sent down for trial from the King's Court at Westminster. It was always possible to remove a case that came before the county court to Westminster for trial by the Justices there. One act of jurisdiction the county courts had beyond even the powers of the courts at Westminster. There was one supreme and solemn act which could be performed only in the county courts and in the folk-moot of the city of London, the act of out-lawry, with all its very serious consequences. The King's Courts at Westminster could indeed order that a man should be outlawed, but the formal ceremony must be done in the county court.

I should like to try to make a session of this mediaeval county court in some way real to you; to do something more than just tell you, as I have done, who was there and, in a very general kind of way, what they did; to tell you something that you are more likely to remember than a string of bare facts. Let us imagine, if you will, that you and I are freeholders of, say, Edward I's time, some-where towards the close of the thirteenth century, and that we are going to attend our county court. What shall we do? What shall we see? What shall we say? To begin with, even supposing that we are very well-to-do people, we shall set out from homes that seem far below our modern standard of comfort and convenience even for people who are not particularly well-to-do. The home where we freeholders of the thirteenth century have break-fasted off bread and any sort of meat that might be available, or off dried fish (if it were a Friday or other fast day and we were good church folk or did not want to run any risk of a visit from the Archdeacon's summoner) with a draught of beer or possibly some sort of wine, for we are centuries away from the days of tea and coffee, is built entirely of timber. Even if we are very well off, county gentlefolk of standing and importance in our neighbourhood, it will not seem, as we look back upon it now with our twentieth century eyes, with the recollection fresh in our minds of the homes we left this morning, as very comfortable, very commodious, either in its construc-tion or in its decoration and furnishing. This thirteenth

century home of ours from which we are setting out
to attend our county court consisted, if, as I have con-
ditioned, we were amongst the well-to-do classes, of an
entrance passage running through the house, with a hall
on one side, a parlour behind, and one or two chambers
above; and on the opposite side a kitchen, pantry and
other offices. A gentleman's house containing three or
four beds was extraordinarily well provided; few probably
had more than two. The walls were commonly bare, without wainscot or even plaster. The few inventories of
furniture that have come down to us show a miserable
deficiency in even the houses of the best country gentlemen. There were no adornments of any sort. From such
a home as that we shall set out on our ride to our county
town; for, I suppose that, if we live, as most of us certainly will do, at some distance from it, we shall be on
horseback. And what sort of a countryside shall we ride
through? One very unlike that which would meet our
eyes if we were making the same journey to-day. For
though hill and valley, plain and winding river remain
unchangeable and unchanged as they were in Edward I's
time, the general prospect that would have lain before
us as we made our journey between six and seven hundred
years ago is very different from the one we should have
seen had we gone that way this morning. There is one
especial feature of the country landscape of to-day that
we should miss at once. There were no green hedges six
hundred years ago dividing field from field. Fences of a
sort indeed there were, rough temporary palisades of
stakes set up while the crops were growing to protect them
from the horses and other cattle, and removed when the
crops were harvested. The characteristic green hedges of
our modern English country landscape come to us mainly

as a consequence of the Enclosure Acts of Queen Anne's reign. We shall notice as we pass along what would seem to twentieth century eyes an excessive amount of arable land, a deficiency of pasture land. But that does not surprise us, because we know that there is a great stretch somewhere of common pasture land available for the use of all the freeholders, whereon each of these may turn a number of heads of cattle proportionate to the amount of his holding. We shall probably see much forest land, for in a country where the use of bricks had been long forgotten and houses and barns and cattle-sheds were built mostly of wood, timber in plenty was very necessary; and the oak and the ash, the elm and the fir are growing abundantly. Many an orchard, too, we shall see, thickly planted with apple and pear trees, but mainly apple trees. We shall not pass any of the trim little cottages we see to-day, with neatly kept gardens gay with flowers. And as we get nearer to our journey's end we shall probably fall in with others who are on the same errand as ourselves; at any rate, when we reach our county town we shall certainly meet many of them there. Perhaps we are parties, ourselves, to some action that is to come before the court. We are, at least, pretty sure, if we are ourselves neither actual plaintiff nor defendant, to be interested in someone who is, a neighbour, a relation. And I suppose that as we have opportunity we shall foregather with such of our fellow freeholders as we have any acquaintance with and try to win their interest and support for the side which is our side—for you will remember that it is with the freeholders that judgment lies, and not with the Sheriff. We shall doubtless explain how entirely right our side is, how wholly in the wrong the man on the other side is. And when we have done all the lobbying which we have been able to do as we rode along and in the high street of our county town, we shall, after stabling our horses and getting some refreshment for ourselves in one of the local taverns, go into the shire hall or wherever the court is summoned to sit. It must, I am afraid, be mainly a matter of inference and surmise what we shall see there. We have ancient illuminations picturing for us the mediaeval courts at Westminster, but I know of no contemporary picture of a mediaeval county court. Still we may form some sort of a serviceable guess of what it was like. There is not room for us to get very widely astray. There is pretty sure to be some sort of a dais or slightly raised platform at one end of the room, on which the Sheriff, with any clerical staff he may bring with him, will sit. The coroners for the county will probably sit there too; and if the Bishop or the Earl or any other of the principal magnates of the county be present, he will probably have his seat there as well. In the body of the hall the freeholders, including the parish priest, will be gathered; and I do not think that there will be any provision of seats for them. Seats in public places were not generally considered necessary in mediaeval days.

I have said that the county court was the great popular court for the ordinary man; the court to which the ordinary man went when he had any grievance which the court had jurisdiction to remedy. I have told you in a general way what kind of cases were triable at the county court. Most of these cases were commenced by what was called a plaint, but some of them had to be tried under a writ. Those writs were to be got only from the Chancery in London; at least all authority seems to make that certain. I have never been able to find out, to understand, how a would-be plaintiff, living, perhaps, a week's journey from London, actually got his writ. To-day, wherever a man lives, there is some local solicitor living within a few miles of him at the most, and that local solicitor has an agent in London to whom he can send instructions to take out a writ; and the business can be completed through the post in a few hours. But how did a man living far away in the country get his writ in Edward I's time? That he could get it and did get it in some reasonably simple way is obvious, but I cannot certainly tell you how. When the General Eyre visited a county there is some good reason for believing that a local chancery was set up where writs were obtainable; but that was an exceptional thing, and we have no reason for supposing that outside the Eyres there was ever anything in the nature of county chanceries. The writ, apparently, could be got in London only.

If we thirteenth century freeholders are going to take any intelligent interest in the proceedings of our county court, if we are going in any real way to understand what is going on, we must be something of linguists. We must at any rate be able to understand the French of the courts, and it will help us if we know a little Latin too. The writ was in Latin, most records and other official documents were in Latin. Some of you may remember how even when the angel came down from heaven, in *Piers the Plowman*, to bear a message to William Langland, that angel delivered his message in Latin; and William's reflection is that so these things were because illiterate people ought not to be told how to justify themselves. All who could not understand Latin or French had best suffer and serve seems to be his pessimistic reflection. But you will probably ask me if I really suppose that all the lesser people, or, indeed, many of the bigger ones, who were suing or being sued or were present as judges in the county court, understood even French, to say nothing about Latin; and I tell you at once that I do not. Considering the method of procedure it was not necessary that they should. The local freeholders who came to determine on which side right lay and to give their judgment accordingly came into court with their judgments already settled in their own minds. They had them in their pockets, as we say to-day. Now do not think that this was a shocking state of affairs. It was a perfectly right state of affairs in the circumstances of the time; and it was almost the only possible state of affairs. These were men on the spot, the men who, if any, knew of their own knowledge or could easily find out by enquiry on the spot all about the litigants, their family history and personal affairs; and if they did their duty, did what public opinion and the legal theory of the time expected them to do, they did find out all that they needed to know in supplement of the knowledge they already had to enable them to come into court ready to register a judgment which they had already made. And I do not suppose that the freeholders who came from the other side of the county troubled themselves at all about the matter at issue. They had no means of knowing anything about it and they left it to those who did know. There was practically the same system and certainly the same theory in the courts at Westminster. There, until both sides had said everything they wanted to say in support of their respective cases, until they had exhausted their quiver of pleas, no jury was present. If in the end the decision had to be left to a jury, twenty-four[1] men were sent up to London from the litigants' county, and they, without their ever having heard a word of the pleading, were

---

[1] Twelve only were needed, but twenty-four were summoned, to provide for casualties during the journey and for challenges at Westminster.

expected to give their verdict for one side or the other simply on their own locally acquired knowledge. What mattered it to them whether they understood or did not understand Latin or French? Under the tuition of the clerk of the court their verdict could be clothed in the necessary formal words. So with our county freeholders. If they could understand their neighbours and their neighbours could understand them, they could get on very well without French or Latin.

But I am perhaps hastening on a little too fast. The time has not yet come for the freeholders to deliver their judgment. They must first listen to the formal pleadings, whether they understand them or not. These pleadings were in Anglo-Norman, and their general forms have been preserved for us by contemporary compilers of collections of precedents. The Latin name for them was *narraciones*, the Anglo-Norman name was "counts"; and in English they seem to have been called "tales." The stories of the plaintiff and the defendant had to be embodied in them, the most scrupulous care being necessary that these stories should be told in the precise form laid down in the precedent. The plaintiff's count usually began in this way—I am turning the Anglo-Norman of the original into its equivalent English: This showeth you *A* who is here that *B* who is there wrongfully does this or that to the detriment of *A*, and wrongfully became, whereas— and then the whole story is set out from *A*'s point of view. Then *B* comes on and tells the story from his own point of view, beginning after much the same form. *A* perhaps replies, and when neither side has anything more to say, the Sheriff asks the freeholders for their judgment, and their judgment is the judgment of the court. If it be for the plaintiff the Sheriff takes the necessary steps to carry it out. The judgment of the free-holders is decisive, though in certain circumstances there is an appeal from it to the courts at Westminster. But time will not let me go into that now, nor speak of the grave inconveniences which arose from time to time from the fact that the judgments of the court were not officially recorded, or of the steps which were taken in certain matters to remedy this inconvenience.

As my subject in these lectures is not the county court I must not say all about it that I should like to say; all that you, perhaps, might be interested in hearing. But I could scarcely tell you the full story of the Eyres from the beginning without saying something of the other and older courts which administered justice in mediaeval England. I have spoken but shortly of the county court, yet I must be even briefer in speaking of the other early English courts. The hundred court met every three weeks. Normally the Sheriff should be the president, or a bailiff to whom the Sheriff had committed the hundred; but, as I have said, many of the hundreds had from time to time been granted by the Sovereign into private hands, and in these cases the steward of the particular manorial lord to whom a hundred had been granted will preside. The freeholders of the hundred owe suit to it. As in the county court they are the judges. Its competence seems much the same as that of the county court, though its powers are, of course, confined within narrower geo-graphical limits; but real actions do not come to it, nor do we hear of actions being transmitted to it from the courts at Westminster. Twice a year the Sheriff makes a tour—the Sheriff's "turn" was the technical name for it—through all the hundreds of his county. He personally holds each of the hundred courts, and on these occasions many things were done which were not done at the ordinary sessions of the court, and many besides the ordinary suitors ought to be present. But into most of this I cannot go now. Just this I will say. One of the objects of the turn was that the Sheriff might hold what we may call a police court; a police court of first instance. The Sheriff, you remember, was a royal officer clothed with a certain amount of the King's power to punish breaches of the King's peace. Presentments were made in this court by representatives of the townships within the hundreds and by juries of the freeholders of crimes and minor offences. The presentments of minor offences were disposed of on the spot. Up to 1217 the Sheriff had power to try charges of felony at his "turn," but that jurisdiction was then withdrawn from him, and the presentments of the more serious crimes merely served to initiate proceedings against the accused which would be tried by the King's Justices at a subsequent Gaol Delivery or during a General Eyre. In his "turn," however, the Sheriff acted as a judge with powers delegated from the King, and it would seem that the freeholders, the suitors of the court, had nothing to do with the judgments.

I will glance now, and it must be very hastily, at the seignorial courts, the Courts Baron. As a result of William I's system of tenures, England after the Norman conquest was covered with the private jurisdictions of lords of various degrees, from the King downwards, holding courts on their lands at which their tenants were entitled to seek justice in their own local affairs, and bound, under penalties which were enforceable by distress levied on their lands, to attend, that they might see that justice was done to their fellows. According to the theories of the time jurisdiction was involved in the mere possession of a manor, or in the mere fact of having tenants. William divided the whole country, except so much as he kept in his own hands, into manors, tenures of one kind and another; and with each of these grants of manors the right to hold a court to enforce the custom of the manor was recognized. These courts were held every three weeks, and the presiding officer was usually the lord's steward; while it was the bailiff's duty to see that all complaints were ready for hearing and to act generally as a sort of public prosecutor. The suitors, as in the county and hundred courts, were the judges. The proceedings were in the Anglo-Norman of the time; and several books of precedents have come down to us in the original manuscript, giving us the forms in which complaints of one kind and another were, or should have been, made and heard. Many of these manorial courts exercised, either legally by royal grant or illegally by usurpation, powers far beyond those naturally inherent in a Court Baron. Some of them exercised, rightly or wrongly, such regalities as view of frank-pledge, correction of infractions of the assize of bread and beer and the like. Some of them adjudicated in actions of debt between tenants. Others used even more extended powers, the power of executing judgment of life and limb; trying felons for capital offences, and giving them but short shrift when they were found guilty. Here is the conclusion of such a case which I read not long ago: "Take him away," said the steward to the bailiff, "and let him see a priest." That was a sufficient form of judgment. No need of further or cruder words. And then the nearest tree, with a stout branch six feet or so above the ground. That was all.

Nothing, perhaps, spurred on the advisers of our mediaeval kings to send out their roving commissions more than did this knowledge that many of the manorial courts (and every inch of the country outside what the King had retained in his own personal possession was within the jurisdiction of one manorial court or another) were exercising these royal powers without any right or warrant, and by such usurpation were depriving the King of very large profits, constantly accruing, and diverting them into the pockets of the lords. I said a little while ago that the legal theory of the time had not arrived at a definite classification of courts. But it was arriving, and by the beginning of Edward I's reign had attained to a definite classification of jurisdictions or jurisdictional rights. The question which was being constantly raised throughout the land was not what courts has the lord by right, not whether he has a court leet, what we may call a police court, as well as a court baron, but what powers has his court, be it called whatever it may be called? Has he view of frank-pledge, assize of bread and beer, infangthief, and so on, or has he merely those rights which flow from tenure? And the General Eyre, with its powers of enquiry into all these questions, was a very effective machine for wringing out answers to them.

Now I want you to put two and two together and see how much they make, and then consider what this system of courts meant to the mediaeval freeholder. He was a freeholder of his county, of his hundred and of his manor. Once a month he was bound to attend his county court; every three weeks he was bound to attend his hundred court and, also every three weeks, he was bound to attend his manorial court. He might, and in most cases, I suppose, did live miles and miles away from the place where his county court met. He probably often lived some considerable way from the place where the hundred court met. Add all these courts together and see what the sum total comes to. It means an attendance at one court or another something very like once a week all the year round. And he might very well be detained at the county court for a couple of days, even, perhaps, longer; and at the hundred court, too. And he had his work at home to do; his ploughing and his sowing and his harvesting to look after; to see that his cattle were properly attended to, that they were driven out to pasture and brought home again; he had a hundred different things to do at home which wanted the master's eye. Yet once a week he had to leave home on a more or less distant errand, not knowing when he would return. And then there was all the expense involved in these ever recurring attendances at court. And besides all this he might be called upon, as many of them certainly were, to go up from the furthest ends of the land to serve on a jury at Westminster, to make the journey there and back at his own expense, and to maintain himself for ten days or a fortnight, may be, in London at his own charges. Have you ever tried to think out, have you ever realized what it meant to be a mediaeval freeholder? Attendance at all these courts must have been a great, a very great burden; and no wonder that we hear now and again of some of them buying themselves off, getting relief from their responsibilities by a payment of money to the King. I daresay that there was often much grumbling when some elderly or busy squire drew on his riding-boots and looked out at the weather and wondered where nightfall would find him and in what kind of quarters. Yes, the burden of it all must have been very great, but I think that it was a burden that was on the whole not unwillingly borne. These people were much attached to their feudal courts. They had insisted on the insertion in the Great Charter of a clause guaranteeing them from royal encroachments, and the knights of the shire and the other larger freeholders were probably more than contented to give their attendance at the county court if thereby they could prevent the King's Justices from interfering in their local litigation.

I have reminded you that the Sheriff was a royal officer, and that much money came into his hands in virtue of his office, for which he had to make strict account. Large sums were received by him from fines and amercements imposed in the county court. Twice a year, at Easter and Michaelmas, he had to go to the Exchequer in London and render his accounts and pay in such moneys as he had collected. But Sheriffs were not always to be trusted on their bare word. And then there was a good deal of suspicion about the proceedings of many of the manorial courts. Many of them, it was acknowledged, had received by the King's own grant power to exercise many regalities, a source of considerable profit, a power which was not inherent in the nature of a manorial court. How many of these courts were assuming these powers without any authority at all? That was a question which was exercising the minds of the King's advisers. How many of these courts were assuming a criminal jurisdiction to which they were not entitled? How many lords were taking fines and amercements, were confiscating to their own profit the lands and chattels of convicted felons, taking escheats, and so on; when they had not the smallest right to do anything of the kind? How much money was being lost every year to the King by illegalities of this kind? And now I am bringing you very near to the first genesis of the Eyre. I am bringing you to the actual be-

ginning of those itinerant judicial commissions out of which
the Eyre grew to what in later times it became; that Eyre
to which the main part of these lectures is to be devoted.
Let me say bluntly at once that the origin and purpose of
the earlier commissions out of which the General Eyre grew,
that the main purpose of the Eyre itself, was not the administration of justice, but the gathering into the King's
exchequer as much money as possible in any way possible.
I do not ask you to accept this statement on my own
authority. I will vouch very credible witnesses to warrant
it, though I think that before I have done you will need
no witness for it beyond the story of bare facts which I
shall tell you. Hear in the first place Bishop Stubbs:
"So intimate," he writes, "is the connexion of judicature
with finance under the Norman kings that we scarcely
need the comments of the historians to guide us to the
conclusion that it was mainly for the sake of the profits
that justice was administered at all"[1]. I will quote Maitland next. "To ascertain and protect the rights of the
Crown is the main object; and it seems almost a by-end
that incidentally crime may thus be discovered and suppressed"[2]. One more witness will be sufficient. Professor
McKechnie in his treatise on *Magna Carta* writes: "The
whole machinery of justice was valued primarily as an
engine for transferring land and money to his [*i.e.* King
John's] treasury"[3].

We gather from the Pipe Rolls that it is to Henry I that
the invention of the system of itinerant justices in England
is due. In 1168 (14 Henry II) a deputation of four Barons
of the Exchequer traversed the country as itinerant
justices and collectors of revenue, but as the terms of

---

[1] *Constitutional History* (5th ed.), I, p. 418.
[2] *Constitutional History of England*, p. 127.   [3] p. 444 (1st ed.).

their commission have not come down to us it is now impossible to say what powers they actually had. Seeing, however, that five years afterwards, in 1173, the whole country was divided, for financial purposes only, into six circuits, we may fairly assume that the deputation of the four barons had a mainly financial purpose. Henry II continued for a time these occasional circuits, but by the Assize of Northampton of 1176, in itself an expansion of the earlier Assize of Clarendon in 1166, he rendered this system of itinerant royal justices permanent and regular. His primary object was undoubtedly financial; but the administration of justice was added as a profitable branch. Time will not allow me to trace the gradual growth of these commissions from their limited beginnings till they expanded into that all-covering commission which granted to the later justices of the Eyre the whole of the powers which lay inherent in the King, powers not only to administer right and justice according to the common law and the statute law of the realm, but if need be for the perfect accomplishment of what was equitable, to go beyond and even contrary to such common and statute law; to draw upon the unlimited and unconditioned powers of a King who was—I am in effect quoting Bracton —God's Vicar on earth with all power to judge between right and wrong, and set where he was to see that each one of his subjects, great and small, should be protected and maintained in all his rights, should have full reparation made to him in aught wherein he had been injured by another. That was the pleasant theory. We shall see what the Eyre became in actual fact. I must pass over all this story of growth and bring you at once to the commission of the General Eyre, the commission to hold pleas of every kind; the commission which invested the justices of the Eyre with practically all the King's powers and jurisdiction, which set them above the law, and made them, we may almost say, kings themselves within the county wherein they were in session.

And here, I think, I ought to tell you how I come to be able to tell you much of what I am going to say about these old Eyres. You will not find very much about them in the legal histories on the shelves of our libraries. Bracton and Britton and Fleta will tell you something about their powers and the forms in which this or that set of people whose duty it was to attend them were summoned, and in some dry way what the justices and sheriffs and coroners and other officials did or ought to do. The Plea Rolls of two or three of them have been transcribed and printed. Partial reports of the Eyres of Hereford and Shropshire of 20 Edward I, of Staffordshire of 21 Edward I and of Cornwall of 30 Edward I are included in the Rolls Series of Year Books, edited by the late Mr Horwood. Only the last named of these gives us even the scantiest report of what happened outside the trial of the cases reported. In the *Liber Custumorum* of the City of London, an excellent edition of which is included in the Rolls Series, we have many valuable details given us of the preliminary proceedings and of much that happened during the progress of the London Eyre of 14 Edward II. But this account was put together mainly from the point of view of the Corporation of the City of London, and deals almost exclusively with matters affecting the citizens in their corporate capacity. Still it is a most valuable and interesting source of information. In the *Liber Albus* of the City of London, which has been printed in the same series, is a sort of manual of general instruction as to what should be done and by whom when a General Eyre for the city is at hand. This was probably compiled at the time of the Eyre of 4 Edward I. It is only some dozen years ago that the manuscript year books of the Eyre of Kent of 6 and 7 Edward II were read and carefully studied and collated. The original compilers of these last named year books have given us not only reports of trials, but have, some of them, set out at great length every detail of all the preliminary procedure before the trial of actions or of pleas of the crown or of the prisoners lying in gaol commenced. The full story of that Eyre is extant in a greater number of contemporary, or nearly contemporary, year books, so far as we know, than that of any other Eyre; and the Selden Society has published in three volumes all that is now ascertainable, outside the record of the Rolls of Eyre, which give little more than formal details of trials, of all that happened during the session of that very long Eyre which seems to have continued, with some vacation during harvest time, at least a full year. Further research has brought to light more or less full year books of other Eyres—by this term I mean manuscripts which give us, besides more reports of the cases tried, details of the general procedure observed, of all the many things which were done and said at a General Eyre outside the trial of actions and prisoners. It is these various manuscript year books of various Eyres held during the reigns of the three Edwards which are my authority for all I am going to tell you. They are, except for such formal details as Bracton and one or two other mediaeval writers give us, our only authorities; and I do not know that Bracton and the others tell us anything which the compilers of these manuscript year books of the Eyres have not told us equally well, and often in a more life-like and spirited way. Our equipment,

then, in the main, is the old year books of the Eyres,
most of them still unprinted, and still generally un-
available for study by historians either of law or of anything else. Our earliest Eyre Rolls date from John's
reign, but these early rolls give us only the barest details,
and are of little or no use for our present purpose, and
they are often only fragmentary; and there is no surviving
year book of an Eyre earlier than that of 20 Edward I
to which I have just made reference, with the possible
exception of some extracts from a perished book of John's
time which have been copied into one of the year books
of Edward I. We must wait till we get to Edward II
before we can speak of the procedure with any fulness.

The first step in the constitution of a commission of
General Eyre was the appointment of four or five justices
to hold it. These justices, important as their work was,
were not exclusively chosen from the King's professional
Justices at Westminster. Two or three of these would
usually be on the commission and another two or three
would be men of position and influence, usually, I think,
Serjeants, but not necessarily belonging to the district
which they were commissioned to itinerate. Bishops and
Abbots were sometimes appointed, and had to serve to
the great scandal of strict churchmen. The notice of the
coming of the Justices was sent to the Sheriff of the
county, or to both Sheriffs in the case of the city of
London. The Eyres were hated by all men, hated and
feared. I will not stop here to explain fully to you why.
That will become apparent by and by. Still it is well
that even at this point you should have in your minds
the effect which the announcement of an Eyre was likely
to have upon those whom it immediately concerned. In
1233 an Eyre for Cornwall was proclaimed. An old

chronicler tells us that upon receipt of the news all the
inhabitants fled into the woods in their dread fear of the
Justices[1]. In 22 Edward III the Commons made it a condition for granting supplies to the King for two years
that during that time Eyres should cease throughout the
Kingdom. In the forty-fifth year of the same reign the
"poor commoners" prayed the King "that he would per-
mit no Eyre to be held in any part of the kingdom during
the war to the troubling and impoverishment of the commons." It was recognized even by the King and his
advisers that no county could endure a General Eyre
oftener than once in seven years. In 1261 the Justices
in Eyre came to Worcester, but the whole county rose
up in angry protest and refused to receive them, because
seven years had not passed since the last Eyre[2]; and an
Eyre in Norfolk in Henry III's time was postponed because
seven years had not elapsed since the previous one[3].
But the longer an Eyre was postponed the more terrible
it was when it really came; and this, too, I shall leave to
prove itself in its proper place. Bearing all this in our
minds we scarcely need the witness of the contemporary
Liber Custumorum of the City of London to realize in some
lively degree the feelings of the Aldermen and citizens
in 1321, the fourteenth year of Edward II, when the
Sheriffs made it known that a General Eyre was shortly
to sit in the Tower. And it was forty-four years since
there had been an Eyre for the city; which meant, and
they knew it full well, that every alleged failure in duty
of any kind throughout all those years would have to be

[1] "Eodem anno (1233) fuerunt itinerantes in Cornubia quorum
metu omnes ad sylvas fugerunt." *Annales Monastici* (Rolls
Series), III, p. 135.
[2] *Annales de Wygorne* (Rolls Series), p. 446.
[3] Close Roll, Henry III, No. 77, m. 9d,

justified, and those who could justify it had been dead, may be, for a couple of score years, or amercement after amercement would be ruthlessly extorted from them. And so we clearly gather that the receipt of the writ made the citizens very unhappy. They could think about nothing else. Day after day they discussed it amongst themselves, holding perpetual conferences and reading over and studying time after time what records they had of the procedure observed in former Eyres. The copy of the "Ordinances of the Eyre," which these citizens of London so anxiously studied in 1321, just six hundred years ago, is probably that which now forms part of the *Liber Albus*, and was, almost as probably, transcribed for this very purpose by or by the direction of Andrew Horn, from an earlier volume still preserved in the Guildhall. And the first thing their studies taught them was that it was the duty of the two aldermen whose wards lie nearest to the Tower to have constructed, at their own personal cost, a strong bench with fit and proper seats. When this was done, they awaited with what equanimity they could the arrival of the King's Justices. But they were not idle and unconcerned the meanwhile. "From this moment the citizens prepared themselves against the King and his Council, and strengthened themselves with good counsel of pleaders, sparing no expense, seeing that the times required it." They had been advised by their book of instructions that the duties of friendship should be generally insisted upon and advocated; and that if, unhappily, there had been any little friction amongst any of them, that friction must be smoothed away. They must all stand together against the common enemy. It is the one thing they are all talking and thinking about, these aldermen

---

[1] *Liber Ordinacionum de Itinere.*

and citizens of six hundred years ago. There is a bad
time in front of them, and they know it, but at any rate
they can all stick together and tell the same tale where
a tale has to be told; and perhaps it had better be
arranged beforehand, so that no variations may give the
Justices an opportunity for disbelieving everybody and
punishing everybody. But in spite of all their careful
study of precedents and anxiety to do what was right
they very speedily found themselves in trouble. They had
gathered that upon receipt of news that the Justices were
on their way to the Tower it was the duty of the Mayor
and Aldermen and Sheriffs to assemble within Barking
Church, now the Church of All Hallows, and from thence
to send six of their number to welcome and salute the
Justices and to ask leave that they themselves might enter
the Tower, safe and secure. The six arrived at the Tower,
where they found the Justices sitting, and made their
formal application, which was formally granted. Now
unfortunately, and this shows some carelessness on the
part of these worried city officials, the Sheriffs stayed
behind in the church; they did not form part of or come
with the deputation of six. As soon as the Justices' commission had been read, and it seems to have been read
very hastily, as such formal documents are apt to be
read, the crier of the Court loudly and repeatedly called
for the Sheriffs. They, unhappily for themselves and for
the whole city of London, were still in Barking Church
with the Mayor and Aldermen, waiting the return of the
deputation which they had sent to get permission for
them to enter the Tower. But now, on receipt of this and
hearing what had happened, the whole churchful, Mayor,
Aldermen, Sheriffs and others, get themselves to the Tower
in a vast hurry, and respectfully salute the King's Justices

of the Eyre. It is but a sorry and frigid response which they get to their civilities. The King's Serjeant Pleader for the Eyre immediately rises in his place. "The Sheriffs," he says, "who ought to be present at the Eyre before all others, ready and prepared to obey the King and his Justices, did not, upon solemn summons made, appear." And thereupon he asks that by way of punishment the Justices shall declare all the city's privileges and franchises, won from time to time by hard bargaining with the King, to be forfeited; seized into the King's hand is the technical expression. The Mayor and Aldermen and other citizens no doubt felt chilled to the marrow, but they made what excuse they could for themselves, pleading the custom at former Eyres. Not a word did the Justices condescend to say in answer to their apologies. But they had a further word, no comforting one, to say to the Sheriffs. "Sheriffs, because you were not here when you were called, you are under judgment," which meant that by and by, when the Justices had settled amongst themselves how large a fine they should impose upon them, they would hear further of the matter. In this unhappy way the Eyre of the City of London of 1321 opened. The spirit of the Eyre as an institution manifests itself at once. To gather all the money possible into the King's exchequer by fines and amercements, by the confiscation of privileges to be afterwards bought back at a large price, was the first purpose of the Eyre. An old chronicler in noting the death of Robert of Sexington, one of Edward I's justices, says of him that through his long tenure of office he accumulated ample possessions for himself, "and filled the King's treasury"[1].

---

[1] *Chronica Maiora* (Rolls Series), IV, p. 34.

I am not here to tell you the story of this Eyre of London nor of any other Eyre in particular. I am to tell you the general story of all Eyres as best I can, and so I must draw my illustrations and incidents from the records of this Eyre or that as will most adequately serve my purpose. And indeed a London Eyre was an exceptional Eyre, dealing with a small area only. A county Eyre had a much wider sweep; it was the Eyre which was generally known of all Englishmen outside the citizens of London. It is of a county Eyre in action that I will try to give you some sort of panoramic picture, with such comments of my own by the way as I may usefully make. The commission of a General Eyre comprehended all judicial commissions. The Justices were empowered to try every kind of civil action and every kind of misdemeanour and crime. But they were empowered to do much more than all this. They were empowered to enquire into the conduct of every local authority in any way responsible for the preservation of the King's peace and for the adequate maintenance and recognition of every right which the King claimed during all the years which had elapsed since the last Eyre; and if any failure were found in any of them then punishment, usually the infliction of a more or less heavy fine, swiftly followed. But weeks before the Justices arrived there was much commotion and perturbation throughout the county; many arrangements had to be made. And the Sheriff had more than his full share of work to do. Some six weeks before the opening of the Eyre he received what was called the writ of common or general summons; and this sets out a fairly full list of the Sheriff's immediate responsibilities. In the first place he has to summon everybody of any particular rank or means within the county to be present at the opening of the Eyre. Then he has to send a similar summons to four of the better-class men and the reeve or provost of every town. A dozen burgesses, too, from every borough are to be summoned. Then he has to find out where now are all who have been Sheriffs since the last Eyre and summon them too to come before the Justices. You will remember that I said just now that there had been no Eyre for the city of London during a space of forty-four years. When the Eyre did at last come along the Sheriffs then in office had to make up a list of all their predecessors during those forty-four years. Some of these would certainly be dead. In such cases the Sheriff must search out their heirs or executors. Even in a county Eyre he had to go back at least seven years. Then the same search had to be made for all who had been coroners since the last Eyre, or for the heirs or executors of such of them as were dead. Then, according to Bracton, somebody, and I do not see who this somebody could be except the Sheriff, has to see that the names of the inhabitants of all the several hundreds into which the county is divided are enrolled in order. And the Sheriff knows, too, that in a certain roundabout fashion a dozen jurors will have to be chosen from each hundred at a very early stage of the Eyre; and the number of hundreds was often great. In Kent, not one of the largest counties, there were seventy. Then this over-worked Sheriff has to see that all business relating to the Pleas of the Crown—of which I will say something later—that has been accumulating since the last Eyre, and all the arrears of pleas and assizes that might, and I suppose ought to have been disposed of by other judges, but had not been, were in readiness to be brought before the Justices of the Eyre, who would make it very uncomfortable for the Sheriff if they found him wanting in any of these many matters. But this is far from all that the Sheriff has to do when the Justices of the Eyre are coming into his county. He must see that proclamation is made in every city and borough and trading-town and in all sorts of other places throughout the county charging all who claim a franchise of any kind, that is the right to exercise, by virtue of some special royal grant, any royal jurisdiction, to exercise powers in their local manorial courts which are not inherent in the nature of those courts, to come before the Justices at the very commencement of the Eyre and prove their right. He has, further than this, to make proclamation summoning all who have cause of complaint against bailiffs or other officials to come and lay their grievance before the Justices, who were always very willing to listen to any sort of complaint from anyone, for if it was established it gave them the always welcome opportunity of fining somebody to the King's profit, and, if it were not established, then more likely than not they would fine the complainant for making a false complaint. Any kind of complaint by anybody was pretty certain, one way or another, to bring grist to the Eyre's mill.

The Sheriff had to do and get done at least all this in the six weeks before the Eyre. By this time we can well imagine that the whole county, knights and freeholders large and small, lords of manors and their stewards and bailiffs, farmers and market-gardeners, shopkeepers, every class of society, was worked up into a state of some ferment and excitement by the perpetual hearing of proclamations and the receiving of summonses to attend the Eyre in this capacity or that, to make returns of one thing or another. All these things must have been the subject of constant discussion amongst them as they met in their local courts, in the market place, as they gathered together on their way to hear Mass on Sundays and holy days, even in the privacy of their own homes, over the table at meal times or as they gathered at evening in the ingle-nooks round the fire. For they knew full well that these were not mere formal proclamations to which they might turn an inattentive ear, summonses which meant nothing very much and might be obeyed or disobeyed as they listed. Disregard of them would have painful consequences. Previous Eyres had left that lesson behind them.

But there were other and in their own way perhaps even more disturbing consequences of the Eyre than these; consequences which affected those who were not hitherto directly touched, the wives and mothers of the county responsible for the regular provision of meals for their husbands and children and servants, for the getting from shop or market all the many things which were needed for the comfortable conduct of the home and the well-being of the family. No fair or market, so the regular proclamation ran, was to be held within the county during the continuance of the Eyre except in the town where the Justices were actually sitting. I do not quite know what the definition of a market might cover, but anyway the facilities for the provision of the ordinary necessaries of life must have been uncomfortably curtailed for very long periods of time. There were shops, I know, of a sort. But I imagine that very little was to be bought at them of the things which were sold at a market. For the privilege of holding a country market was highly valued by those manorial lords who had the privilege of holding them within their manors. It was a

privilege for which they had probably paid a big price to
the King. Their profits from them in stallage rents and
tolls were large, and anything, like private shop-keeping,
that interfered with their profits, or with the like profits
of the King where the market was a royal one, would have
been, I imagine, promptly suppressed; and so I do not
think that what were called shops would help much.
Outside the county town there must have been something
of the feeling of a secular interdict oppressing the land.

Here alone we might find a sufficient reason, if there
were no others, for the unpopularity of Eyres. The same
Statute[1] which empowered the Justices to issue their
proclamation suspending markets and fairs empowered
them also to command that no hostelry, that is to say
no lodging accommodation, should be hired out, but be
granted freely to them that come. What exactly did this
mean? One can scarcely suppose that it meant that
anyone had a right to walk into any house that attracted
his fancy and demand free lodging there. Perhaps the
real meaning of the statutory provision is to be gathered
from an Inspeximus and Confirmation of a charter of
liberties to the city of York of 5 Edward II, printed in
the Calendar of Charter Rolls of that year (p. 107) which
runs: "No Marshal of the King's Justices in Eyre at
York shall assign to anyone any of the houses of Lodgings
in the city or suburbs during the Eyre of the said Justices
against the will of the owners of the said houses and
lodgings, saving for the Justices themselves and their
necessary servants." I think that we may infer from this
that the real effect of the Statute was to give the Justices'
Marshals power, in the absence of any special privilege

---

[1] *Statutum de sacramento Ministrorum Regis* (Statutes of the
Realm, I, p. 232).

such as was granted to the citizens of York, to billet those whose business or duty brought them to the town in which the Eyre was in session wherever they thought fit.

The session of a General Eyre had yet another consequence of importance. As soon as the Justices had opened their commission and had so become fulfilled of their office, all other judicial commissions that might then happen to be sitting within the county for the trying of assizes or other pleas of any sort whatsoever, for delivering gaols or for aught else, fell straightway and automatically into abeyance. So also did the powers and jurisdiction of the permanent courts within the county. Save for dealing with certain strictly defined matters the work of county court and hundred court was stayed as soon as the Justices of the Eyre had declared the purposes of their coming. The Eyre was for the time being both county court and hundred court. But the influence of the Eyre reached beyond the limits of the county. The Courts at Westminster were estopped from dealing with any business that touched interests in the county wherein the Justices were sitting. If any such action had already been commenced and partly heard at Westminster, a transcript of the pleadings and process, so far as they had gone, had to be sent to the Justices of the Eyre, before whom the hearing would be continued from the point at which it was broken off at Westminster. No court, no judge might do aught that should detract from the solitary supremacy of the Eyre over all persons and all causes, not strictly ecclesiastical, within and touching the county.

Lecture II

I SAID last week that we had more abundant and fuller chronicles of the Eyre of Kent of 1313 than of any other Eyre. From this particular Eyre we can, then, perhaps, draw our best and most instructive picture of Eyres in general. They all followed the same forms—there was even what we may call a stereotyped form of opening speech by the presiding Justice, supposed to have been originally written by Martin Pateshull, a Justice of the Bench who went many Eyres in Henry III's reign and died Dean of St Paul's in 1229. They all did the same business in very much the same way. Only the setting varied. Let us go back, then, in imagination to that Sunday morning, that fell on the first day of July, 1313, towards the close of the sixth year of Edward II, and suppose ourselves in Canterbury. The Sheriff, it is to be hoped, has duly done everything which he ought to do. He knows that presently he will be called to strict account by the Justices and that no excuses will avail him if in aught he be found wanting. The citizens, for whom during several weeks past the Eyre and the coming of the Justices and their personal reputation and character have been the chief topic of conversation and anxious interest, are crowding the streets on this summer Sunday morning to see all that is to be seen. Exactly how the Justices came to Canterbury no record that I know of tells us. But when we remember with what respectful ceremony, even down to our own time, the King's Justices have ever been received in the county towns where they have gone

on their commission of assizes and the rest, and how they
pass through the streets to their Court with escort of
javelin men and fanfare of trumpets, we may be sure that
in those far-off days steeped in the mediaeval love of
pageantry and solemn circumstance these Justices of the
Eyre, who were clothed with much more of the inherent
powers of a King that was above the law than even are
the itinerant Justices to-day with those of a King that is
within the law, were received at the boundary of the
county with every sign of respect; that they rode on
towards Canterbury surrounded by a gallant escort of
nobles and knights, with shimmer of steel and blare
of brazen trumpet and harsh roar of horn and bright
colour of streaming pennon. Gossiping groups of men and
women, boys and girls, no doubt watched them curiously
as they passed along and guessed who each might be.
Let us ride on with the Justices and their escort and see
what happens. On this particular occasion the Chief
Justice of the Eyre, we may note, was Hervey of Stanton,
who acquired for himself amongst the lawyers of his time
the nickname of Hervey the Hasty. He was an eccle-
siastic, a prebendary of York, and held at least one rectory,
and became afterwards Chancellor of the Exchequer, and,
later, Chief Justice of the King's Bench. On this Sunday
morning, six hundred and eight years ago, the five
Justices of Eyre rode into Canterbury and took their seats
in the great hall of the palace and opened their commission. And you will note from this that the mediaeval
courts sat on Sundays. There is plentiful evidence of this
practice to be found elsewhere. I would not have chosen
Canterbury as the scene of our typical Eyre if I had had
a wider choice; but I think that fuller details of the Kent
Eyre of 1313 have come down to us than of any other

Eyre. Except for this constraining reason I should have chosen some other place, some less exceptional place, for Canterbury in the middle ages was a quite exceptional place. The Throne of the Primate of All England was there. The Shrine of the martyred St Thomas, by far the most frequented shrine in England, one of the most frequented in all Europe was there, as well as the shrine and tombs of many a lesser saint. There was the great Abbey of St Augustine, the great Priory of Christchurch, besides five smaller religious houses, nine hospitals and other less important endowments. The city itself was the great thoroughfare to the continent. By reason of all this its streets were no doubt often thronged with princes and nobles, with ecclesiastics of all orders and ranks, with pilgrims and with travellers going their way to and from the channel ports on all sorts of secular business. Somner tells us that in 1320, on the one hundred and fiftieth anniversary of the consecration of Archbishop Becket's shrine, a hundred thousand people were gathered together in Canterbury. Yes, Canterbury was an exceptional place. In Canterbury we can very well understand that there was, that there must necessarily have been, accommodation of all sorts greatly in excess of what was needed for the housing and other requirements of the city's own permanent inhabitants. And so, in the case of Canterbury, this question of finding accommodation and food for all the great number of people whom the Eyre brought into the town where it was sitting does not seem to us so difficult of solution as it appears to be in places like Bedford and Derby. How many people had necessarily to come to an Eyre? Let us look into the records of our Canterbury Eyre, and see what we are told. There were some seventy localities each sending twelve jurors, of whom I shall have more to say presently. These 70 localities included the hundreds, the cities of Canterbury and Rochester and two or three other jurisdictions. That gives us 840 jurors. Then there are four men and the reeve from every town within the county. How many so-called towns were there in Kent in 1313? Lambard wrote his *Peregrination of Kent* in 1570. He describes 145 places as towns. There are very many places to the names of which he affixes no description at all. According to his calendar there are twenty-seven hundreds which contain no "town" at all. Was such really the fact, or was Lambard a little haphazard in his methods? Anyway, I think that we shall not be making an excessive estimate if we suppose that in 1313 there were at least a hundred "towns" in Kent, each sending its reeve and four men to Canterbury, five hundred in all. Then we have all the great people of the county as enumerated in the General Summons of the Eyre. The number of these we can scarcely guess at. We must remember next that the Eyre was attended by the full county court in its corporate capacity. Then there were ex-sheriffs or their representatives, coroners, ex-coroners or the representatives of these, serjeants, attorneys, bailiffs, parties to actions, claimants of franchises, and doubtless many another. Canterbury was used to receiving great crowds of visitors; but where in the smaller county towns, in places like Bodmin or Bedford, was accommodation found for anything like so many people and for the troops of horses, in numbers which I will not attempt to calculate, which most of them must have ridden into the town? The Justices' power of billeting must certainly have been strained to its utmost. But it was not only accommodation for board and lodging and stabling that was needed and was, I suppose, got somehow. It would seem as though the whole of a town where a General Eyre was in session must have been a honey-comb of what we may call committee rooms. There were in Kent, as I have said, some seventy hundreds. Somewhere in Canterbury there must have been some seventy committee rooms, where the twelve jurors of each of the seventy hundreds were taking that counsel with the four men and the reeve from each town within their hundred of which I will tell you by and by. Where and after what manner did all these hold their councils and talk over matters and try to remember all which it was very necessary for their own weal that they should remember? Did they gather themselves in groups in the nave of the Cathedral; did they, for it was full summer time, seat themselves under the shadow of some great tree in the grass land outside the city? Were the cloisters or common rooms of the religious houses open to them? One might go on guessing, but in mere guessing it must end. Somewhere or other and somehow or other the dozens from the hundreds and the men from the towns did come together, must have come together; and there I must leave it. But from any picture you may form in your minds of Canterbury in those summer days of 1313 you must not leave out these many groups of hurried and flustered men, nervously trying to collect and reduce to writing every item in the history of their respective hundreds, the omission of any one of which, they know full well, will mean stern judgment upon themselves by and by.

Let us now go back to our Justices whom we left opening their commission. This commission was an all comprehensive one, giving the Justices power to hear and determine pleas of every kind, to amerce—and here came the sting of the Eyre—all persons whatsoever who have given cause of complaint. The King's will, the Chief Justice said in conclusion, was that all evil-doers should be punished after their deserts, and that justice should be ministered indifferently as well to poor as to rich; and, for the better accomplishing of this, he prayed the community of the county by their attendance there to lend their aid in the establishing of a happy and certain peace that should be both for the honour of the realm and for their own welfare. Then the Sheriff was immediately called and told to produce his writ. The Sheriff of Kent, more fortunate than his colleagues of London of whom I have told you, was happily present and promptly produced his writ which was read aloud in Court. This was the writ giving him the multifarious instructions and commands which I have already summarized for you. Then came the first assumption by the Chief Justice of regal authority. The Sheriff was a royal officer dismissible by the King only. The first official act which Hervey of Stanton does is to order the Sheriff to surrender his wand of office. This was tantamount to dismissing him. Then, after receiving much good advice, he was re-sworn and formally re-installed in his office. And from this, says the chronicler, you shall note that the Sheriff is removable at the will of the Justices in Eyre. Then the real work of the Eyre begins. The Sheriff makes his formal return of the names of all who had been Sheriffs, of all who had been coroners, since the last Eyre, or of the heirs or executors of such of them as were dead. Then these past Sheriffs or their heirs were called upon one by one to deliver up their rolls of office, each one the roll of his own shrievalty, in his own bag. Well for them if they were there to do it. In that case, and if they had their rolls ready the Chief Justice merely affixed his seal to the bag in a way which prevented it being opened without his knowledge and restored it. If they had not their rolls with them ready for delivery, they were promptly given into the custody of the actual Sheriff, who was charged to seize their lands into the King's hands; and the unhappy defaulters themselves were ordered to produce their rolls the next day, "yet saving the right of the King": an expression which means that though their lands might be restored to them, yet they would have to redeem them by the payment of an amercement to the King, the amount being fixed at the discretion of the Justices. But though it was well for these ex-sheriffs to be ready with their rolls it was not well for them to be over-ready. William de Leyre had been one of the Sheriffs of London thirty years before the London Eyre of 1321, and was therefore at the time of the Eyre probably an old man, somewhat flustered and nervous. He, in his excitement, offered his rolls before they were asked for, and, poor fellow, when they were actually asked for, could not for the moment find them. And he was thereupon amerced. Then came the turn of the coroners or their heirs. If they had their rolls, well and good. If they could not show them, promptly the order went to the Sheriff to seize their lands and goods. "And as touching such coroners or their heirs or executors as were called and did not appear, in respect of them the Sheriff was ordered to arrest their persons, to seize their lands and tenements, and turn out their wives and children." Supposing some of the deceased coroners had no representatives who could be made answerable, and had left no lands or tenements behind them, what then? The King was going to be no loser by any unfortunate accident of this kind. The whole county was made responsible for their default and had to pay whatever amercement the Court chose to inflict. And we are told that the reason for this was that the county had chosen these men at its own peril. A prudent county would only choose wealthy men whose estates were sufficiently able to pay. "Since," the Chief Justice said, "they chose one who had not the necessary qualifications, let the whole county be responsible to the King; and let the whole county await judgment." Let me give you one special instance of the harshness with which the Justices used their powers in this connexion. A coroner had died, leaving an infant son and heir. The infant was in the guardianship of some relation who came into Court and said that the rolls of the deceased coroner were in the possession of a certain woman who was his executrix and held them as such. This woman had not been summoned to attend the Court and was naturally not present. But the Justices at once ordered the Sheriff to seize her lands and chattels and to arrest the woman herself and bring her before them the next day, having the rolls with her. This business took up pretty well the whole of the first day of an Eyre; and this first day's business alone will give you sufficient reason for understanding why the Eyre was not a popular institution.

One of the next things to which the Justices gave their attention was the quality and the price of the wine and beer sold within their jurisdiction. The over-worked Sheriff was called before them and told to pick out the two knights and two serjeants who knew most about these matters and bring them before the Court. And when these four men came they were sworn faithfully to acquit themselves of whatsoever they should be charged with in the King's name; and then they were ordered to make a thorough perambulation of the city and search all the taverns and make trial of all the wine and beer they found in them. What they adjudged to be of good quality they were to leave undisturbed; but the casks containing musty liquor they were to have carried out into the street and their contents poured into the gutter. Now mediaeval England was very plentifully supplied with wine and beer taverns, and places like the city of London and the city of Canterbury, continually thronged, as it was, with pilgrims from all over the country to the shrine of St Thomas, were even more generously supplied than the average town. Imagine these four worthy gentlemen going about from tavern to tavern in London or Canterbury till they had visited them all, sampling in each single one of them, as they had made solemn oath that they would do, the contents of every single cask; and then imagine, if you can, the condition in which they must have been at the end of their day's work. However, they had to appear in Court the next day and make a report of their work in many other matters besides this of wine and beer tasting. Besides tasting them it was their duty to formulate a list of prices, known as an assize, at which they were to be sold during the session of the Eyre, and any tavern-keeper who exceeded these prices was severely punished upon conviction. But this commission of four had not only to test the quality and assess the price of beer and wine, but they had to draw up a list of the maximum prices which might be charged for food of all sorts. It may interest you to hear the details of this assessment of prices made in Canterbury in the summer of 1313. The price of a quarter of wheat was fixed at 6s., of oats at 3s.; a whole ox of the best quality at 13s. 4d., a whole sheep of the best quality at 18d., a calf at 2s., a whole pig of the best quality at 4s., a sucking-pig of the best quality at 7d., a fowl of the best quality at 2d., a chicken 1d., a capon 4d., a fat goose 4d., a lean goose 3d., a gallon of the best wine 3d., a gallon of good beer 1d.; and when any of these should be of a quality less good than the best, then they were to be sold at a less price. As far as I know these prices were accepted by the local traders as fair ones, as prices at which they were contented to sell their goods. But this was not always and everywhere the case. In London in 1314 the assessors had fixed the price of a capon of the best quality at 3d., of one of the second quality at $2\frac{1}{2}d$.; of a fowl of the best quality at 2d., of an inferior quality at 1d., a fat chicken at 1d., a goose of the best quality at 4d. These were about the same prices as those assessed at Canterbury, except that the value put upon a capon in London was a penny less than the Canterbury assessment. Eggs were to be sold in London at 6d. the long hundred of 120. Even in those days a pheasant was a relatively costly luxury, being priced at a shilling. These London prices, however, caused much dissatisfaction amongst the city poulterers. According to one account they promptly shut up their shops and refused to do any further business. According to another, they disregarded the assize and fixed their own prices. Probably some did the one and some did the other. It was never a wise thing to flout the Justices of the Eyre. The immediate consequence of the poulterers' action was the arrest of the whole lot of them. They were at once brought before the Justices who straightway sent them all to prison. And so there was not a fowl or an egg to be bought in all the city of London at any price at all. Then, I suppose, the Justices began to reflect. They, like every one else, would have to go without capons and ducks. And the reflection was not, perhaps, an altogether pleasing one. And so, of their special grace, they allowed these unhappy poulterers to go bail, one for another, for their appearance before the Court later on for judgment, on condition that they should henceforth sell at the assessed prices. But the poulterers plead that poultry is very dear and they say that they cannot possibly supply the public at the assessed prices, and they pray that these prices may be revised. This appeal seems to have softened, but only very slightly, the hearts of the Justices. They allowed the prices to be revised to some extent; for instance, the prices allowed for capons and fowls were increased by a halfpenny; that of a pheasant by a penny; eggs were to be sixteen a penny; and so on. But this new tariff was to be in force for only about a week, after which the previous one must be observed. But even with the amended prices the poulterers did not see their way to making anything out of carrying on business; for "after this," the chronicler tells us, "there arose a great dearth and scarcity in the City, because the poulterers could not possibly buy fowls in the country villages for any such prices as those mentioned." The next step was that some set of people, I cannot tell you exactly who they were, probably the Mayor and Aldermen, laid the state of affairs before the King, and prayed him to interfere in such way as would restore to them their accustomed capons and other delicacies. And the King inclined a gracious ear to the petition. He addressed a letter to the Justices saying that it had been brought to his notice that by reason of the royal presence in London and the fact that the royal palaces were there a great multitude of the more important people of the realm and others were always gathered there, and that much inconvenience was caused to all these by the poulterers having ceased to sell poultry because of the low prices allowed by the Justices. And then he goes on to say that, desiring that food of this kind should be had again in abundance, of his own special grace he wills and ordains that henceforward the dealers may sell their wares at a reasonable price, notwithstanding any assessment made by the Justices, whom he commands to issue a proclamation to this effect. And that was the end of the matter; and I do not find any record of the poulterers having been further punished for their original misdoings.

These preliminary matters being cleared off, the Justices turned their attention to a more serious part of the business of the Eyre, the Pleas of the Crown, embodied in what were called the Articles of the Eyre. It was these Pleas of the Crown that more than aught else made the Eyre hateful in the sight of all men, a visitation which no county might endure oftener than once in seven years. One might write a whole volume, and no short one either, on the origin and growth of the Articles of the Eyre. I must deal with them here as briefly as is consistent with making this part of my subject intelligible to you. These Articles formed, in effect, a long catechism demanding information on every sort of matter where a possible answer might afford ground for extracting an amercement from somebody, for forcing somebody to pay a fine to the King to avoid worse things. Comparatively few in their beginning, they were, as Eyre succeeded Eyre, being continually increased in number. The cast of the net was ever widening, the meshes ever narrowing. Great and small were caught in it. "Under the pretext of administering justice," Matthew Paris wrote in the first half of the fourteenth century, "they (*i.e.* the Justices of the Eyre) harvest an infinite sum of money for the King's use"[1]. Before saying more of these Articles I had better tell you how the enquiries under them were worked and describe shortly the machinery of this dreaded inquisition. On an early day of the Eyre the bailiffs of all the hundreds, or wapentakes as they were called in some counties—in the London Eyre the wards represented the county hundreds—were summoned to appear before the Justices and each was sworn to choose two good men and true, the best fitted for the purpose, through whom the truth might be best discovered. I may just note here that if any of these bailiffs failed to appear, immediate order was given to the Sheriff that he should seize all their lands and chattels, eject their wives and children from their home, and arrest the defaulting bailiffs themselves and bring them before the Justices. This, however, is a mere incident. The same fate awaited everyone who failed to obey a summons to appear in court; and so I need not mention it again. You will take it as happening as a matter of course. When the bailiffs had chosen two substantial people, usually knights, from their several hundreds, the Justices called for those so chosen to come before them. And then to each of them separately an oath was administered commencing with these words: "Hear this, ye Justices. Faithfully will I choose of myself and the others of my hundred sixteen good men and true that be best informed and that truth will tell." These electors then went away and each pair of them chose sixteen, in which sixteen they might include themselves. By some process or other of which I know

[1] *Chronica Maiora* (Rolls Series), IV, p. 34.

no detailed account, only that what was done was done outside the Court, four names were struck off each panel, leaving twelve on it. And these twelve men whose names remained on the panel constituted what was called "the dozen" of the hundred. These were the men who had to answer, in respect of their own hundreds, the countless questions contained in the Articles of the Eyre. What within reasonable limits can I say to you about these Articles? Without rehearsing them in full I can scarcely give you any adequate notion, and to do that would leave me no time to say anything else to you to-day. They demanded of the dozens a complete knowledge of every breach of the law, both criminal and civil, of every crime and tort, of every act, one may say, that fell short of absolute blamelessness, that had happened since the last Eyre. Is there one in their hundred that has made a trespass on the high road, that has taken a trout from a river in unorthodox fashion, has opened a market where he had no business to open one—I am mentioning only minor matters—or has done any one of the hundreds of things suggested in the Articles. Then let the dozen be sure that they remember it. They will be amerced for any omission when the Justices detect it, and detect it they almost certainly will, for they have all the county records before them. And while they must be sure that they forget nothing, they must try to make it equally sure that every tittle of what they say is neither more nor less than the exact truth, for fines and amercements await any variation from provable historical fact. But, in their anxiety lest they should forget anything that they ought to say, let them beware of saying anything that they are not invited to say, for trouble lies that way too. Little wonder that certain Yorkshiremen once preferred to pay the King the large sum of £100 rather than risk all the perils that beset the way of a dozen through the Eyre[1]. Copies of these Articles as they were promulgated at different times may be found in certain printed books. The earliest we know, those of 1194 and those of 1198 may be read in Hoveden's *Chronicle*. The Kent Articles of 11 Henry III are in Bracton; those of the London Eyre of 1244 are printed in the *Liber Albus*, as also are those of the London Eyre of 1321. The Articles of 1321 are fully seven times as long as those of 1244; a fact from which you may learn something of the unhappy way these Articles had of widening their sweep, becoming more microscopic in their examinations, as time went on. A transcript of the Articles of the Kent Eyre of 1313 is printed in the Selden Society's edition of the Year Books of that Eyre. Copies of some other sets of Articles have been printed elsewhere, but what I have said is sufficient for our present purpose. All the texts of these Articles that have come down to us are in Latin, but it would appear that they were rehearsed to the dozens in English. And they were not only read to them in English, but they were explained to them by the Chief Justice. All the dozens of the whole county were present in Court during this reading and explanation, everyone else being ordered to withdraw. After the reading and explanation of the Articles, a copy of them is given to each several dozen—I cannot tell you certainly in what language—and then they are told to go away and make their answers in writing. And for their copy of the Articles each dozen has to pay four shillings to the clerk of the Court, and four shillings in those days was the equivalent of at least as many pounds to-day.

[1] Pipe Roll of Henry I, p. 34.

How were these unhappy men to make a sufficient answer to all the countless questions that were addressed to them? Even if they could remember the more serious happenings in their hundred since the last Eyre, how were they to remember, even if they had ever heard of them, of such trifles as the omission of young men with the necessary qualification in land to get themselves knighted when they came of age, or the fact that somebody had sent horses or dogs to a monastery to be fed there at the monks' cost? These men on the dozens had not been keeping detailed diaries these many years past in anticipation of an Eyre. They have, indeed, the assistance of the four men and the reeve from every town. These may be expected to know something of their own local affairs, and they are there for the especial purpose of putting their local knowledge at the service of the dozen of their hundred. An inspection of the coroner's rolls, containing pretty full information about many matters, would have been worth much to them. But these were out of their reach, being in their respective bags sealed with the Chief Justice's seal, and the Chief Justice took care that no tricks should be played with them. He kept the rolls in his own custody during the day for the information of the Court, and re-sealed them every evening, and was careful in the morning to see that there had been no tampering with his seal. Now and again those who knew that they were going to be chosen on dozens had taken time by the forelock and persuaded coroners to let them see their rolls. But unhappy were such coroners when coroner after coroner was questioned by the Court: "By the oath which you have taken, have you given anyone a copy of your rolls since you were summoned to the Eyre?" And some of them acknowledged that they had. "Then for that you will await our judgment." And that meant more money into the King's pocket. The dozens had two or three days to ponder over all these things and then they had to make return of their answers. And that return, they were told, was to be written on a roll, and to each article they were to make a several reply. As to such an Article they were to say so and so; and as to such another they were to say that they had no information. And this return of answers was to be made in French. At the appointed time each dozen came into Court separately, and the Chief Clerk of the Crown took up that dozen's roll and read the present-ments as they were there written, in French. Then he made the dozen make their presentments all over again, but this time in English. "And neither disagreement with, nor aught contrary to, their first presentation must there be; and if there were, then the judgment was that they must go to prison till they had made fine with the King." The dozen was now well started on its thorny way. "But," the Justices added, "since we shall want you presently, you need not go to prison if you pay your fine." Much money was going to be got through the information to be supplied by the dozens, and so they must be kept in Court to supply that information and to find verdicts founded upon it. Of course I cannot take you through a hundredth part of the multifarious matters these dozens presented to the Court. Even in the rolls of the Court I should imagine that they are much summarized and abbreviated. But something of them I must say, or my story of the Eyre would be sadly incomplete. And for your better understanding of these presentments by the dozens I ought to tell you something of one or two other matters to which these presentments make frequent reference. I must take you back for a moment to the days of King Canute the Dane. The Danes who came over with him had not, I gather, made themselves very popular with the English, and when Canute was about to leave England for a time, fearing that the English might take advantage of his absence to oppress or destroy his own Danish subjects, he enacted a law that, when any person was killed and the slayer escaped, the person killed should always be considered a Dane, unless proved to be English by his friends or relations, and a heavy fine exacted from the neighbourhood. This law was adopted by William I in favour of his own subjects. He ordained that where a Frenchman was secretly killed and the people of the hundred had not arrested the slayer and brought him to justice within eight days, they should pay a fine of forty-seven marks, and every person secretly slain was to be held a Frenchman unless it was specifically proved that he was an Englishman. Consequently it was necessary, if the neighbourhood in which a man had been killed (and the slayer had got away undetected) were to escape the infliction of this fine this proof must be given. Its technical name was Englishry, and the name of the fine inflicted in absence of this proof was *murdrum*. A common entry in the old rolls is: Englishry not presented, therefore murder. Murder had a quite different meaning in those days from that which it carries to-day. It was then the name of a fine and not the name of a crime. We see from the terms of the General Summons of the Eyre that the full county court was there present in what we may call its corporate capacity; and at an early stage of the Eyre, before the Pleas of the Crown were heard, the full county court was called before the Justices and bidden to declare whether Englishry had been or ought to be presented within their county. Now this is a matter about which, one would think, no set of intelligent men could have been in any doubt. The very smallest inquiry would surely have discovered the truth to them; and they knew quite well—at least it is hard to believe that they did not—what the consequence of saying the thing that was not would be; and the Justices had the record of the last Eyre before them. They had also before them the Coroners' Rolls. Furthermore, it was almost the unbroken rule at this time throughout England that Englishry should be presented. There were very few exceptions. Yet in county after county we find the freeholders declaring with the utmost assurance that Englishry ought not to be presented within their county and never had been. Then the Chief Justice would certainly speak somewhat in this wise: "Sirs, because you have told us that Englishry should not be presented in this county and we see from the roll of the last Eyre that it should be presented, we put the whole county under judgment." And then, I suppose, some sort of cold shudder ran down the freeholders' backs, but they never ventured to argue the matter further. Englishry was proved in somewhat different ways in different counties, but it seems usually to have been proved by two witnesses on the father's side and two on the mother's. These witnesses went before the coroner and proved that the slain man was of their blood. It was also the duty of the person who first discovered the body of a slain man and the four nearest neighbours of the same to go at once to the coroner and give what information they could. If there was no entry on the coroner's roll that they had done this, so much the worse for them when the Justices of Eyre came and looked into matters.

There is one other technical term about which I had better say something before we listen to some of the presentments which the dozens are going to present to the Justices. To-day we read of coroners' inquests finding verdicts of accidental death. The old phrase was death by misadventure. When a man met his death by mis-adventure or by accident, as we say to-day, some thing was connected with the accident which in some vague sort of way might be considered the cause of it. A man stands on the wheel of a cart to gather berries from a tall bush. He slips, falls and breaks his neck. The wheel was held to be in some sort of way the cause of the man's death, and as such was said to be forfeit to God—*deodand*. The technical rule in settling what was and what was not deodand, and so forfeited as deodand to the King, was laid down in these terms. "Everything that moves along with that particular thing which is the agent of a man's death is deodand to the King." In the case which I have just supposed of a man falling from the wheel of his cart, the cart itself must be taken as remaining itself quite stationary. If it had appeared at the inquest that the horse had moved the cart at the time, then the whole cart and its contents and the horse or horses drawing it would have been forfeited, the whole loss falling upon the owner, who was not in the smallest degree to blame for what had happened. Again, a man falls into a vessel of boiling water and is scalded to death. Here it is the vessel which is deodand and forfeited to the King. But if a pig overturns a pan of boiling water over a little lad and the lad is so scalded that he dies, both the pig and the pan are deodand. A man is felling a tree. The tree, in its fall, strikes another tree and breaks off a branch from it. This branch falls upon the man and kills him.

What is deodand in these circumstances? It was determined that the whole of the first tree and the branch,
but the branch only, of the second tree were. Fine
questions sometimes arose, and much subtlety of reason-
ing was brought into play in settling them. When it is
settled what is actually deodand, the coroner's jury has
to determine its value, and the Sheriff is responsible for
seeing that that value is paid into the Exchequer. He
has, I suppose, to sell them for that sum. It may occur
to you that in such a case as I have imagined where a
farmer loses his cart and its contents and perhaps a team
of two or four horses just because his carter has done
something which he ought not to have done, the coroner's
jury would put merely a nominal value upon them, that
the owner might redeem them at that small price. But
they dare not do that. The Justices of the Eyre when
they come along, perhaps years afterwards, go into all
these matters; and if a jury is found to have undervalued
a deodand, then that jury is brought under judgment.
The usual custom was, I think, that the King should
devote the money accruing to him from the sale of
deodands to some religious or charitable purpose. That,
at any rate, was the theory; and there is actually in
existence an order from Edward II to the Justices of the
Eyre of Kent of 1313 directing that Adam of Osgodby,
the Keeper of the House of *Conversi* in London shall have
"the King's alms called deodands" from their Eyre, in
aid of the repair and maintenance of the buildings of the
Conversi and the maintenance of the *Conversi* themselves.
There is a note in several of the old manuscripts that
deodands which do not exceed sixpence-halfpenny in
value are the perquisite of the Clerk of the Crown.

But we have kept the dozens waiting long enough. The

first one to be called is facing the Justices, in no happy frame of mind, we may be sure, as they await the wearily long catechism which they know is going to be propounded to them question after question, and sadly conscious that any slip they may make will have the most painful consequences for them. Listen to this, and the dozens knew it full well. "The dozens shall come and put in their replies to the Articles and also to the indictments, private matters, felonies, homicides and robberies and all other felonies committed since the last Eyre; and if the Justices find any variance between the rolls of the Coroners and the rolls of the dozens, or find that the dozens omit matters presented by the Coroners, then shall the dozen in fault be under judgment, that is to say amerced; and if any dozen shall assess the chattels of a felon, convicted or fugitive, at a less value than they are assessed at in the Coroner's roll, or shall present fewer persons as being concerned in any particular felony than are found to be charged therewith in the Coroner's roll, they shall be similarly dealt with, and this for conceal- ment." But it was worse than this in reality. Not only were the dozens responsible at their peril for making a flawless report, a report to which no exception could be made, of all these matters which had occurred since the last Eyre, but they were equally responsible for reporting all like matters which had occurred between the last Eyre and the Eyre before that one and had not been finally disposed of at the last Eyre. And the least slip or omission brought them under the judgment of the Court. Can you wonder if they felt, to use the old reporter's simile, as though they stood defenceless before lions ready to rush on their prey? You want no further words of mine to make you understand why these men of long ago hated and feared the Eyre more perhaps than they hated and feared aught else.

I find myself shivering, so to speak, at the brink of these presentments, very much as I am sure the dozens did; hesitating to take the plunge, for it seems so hopeless within the limits of a lecture to give you an intelligent understanding of all they were, of all they meant and involved. Perhaps I can best do all that is possible within my limitations by giving you some of the presentments actually made, and the consequences of them. Many presentments involved charges of felony; many did not. We will deal with this latter class first, as the procedure followed in the two classes differed. The first presentment I shall quote is interesting as showing an early instance of the King's common law power to impress his subjects for war service outside the kingdom. It comes from the Kent Eyre of 6 Edward II. The dozen presented that R. Grace and certain who consorted with him had killed a certain man within the city of Canterbury and had then surrendered themselves to the King's peace. Afterwards the King, then being in Gascony, sent his writ to the bailiffs of the said city charging them to send to him the said R. and his companions; and this they did. Let me interpolate here that anyone who had the custody of anyone charged with any offence and allowed him to escape from that custody, was liable to punishment by the Justices of the Eyre. Now I will go on with the presentment, or the enrolment of it. "But those bailiffs are now dead, and the bailiffs that be have no writ from the King. Therefore there must be judgment of them for escape of the aforesaid prisoners." Consider what that means. Years and years before the Eyre the King orders by his writ that certain persons, lying under a charge of felony, are to be sent to him in France. That writ would have been a complete protection to the bailiffs to whom it had been sent if the Eyre had been held at a time at which it was producible. But years elapse before another Eyre comes. The bailiffs who had the custody of the prisoners are dead. The King's writ to them has disappeared. The present bailiffs know nothing about it, and were in no way concerned in the matter. But the Justices find that certain persons were consigned to the custody of the bailiffs of Canterbury. They are wanted now for trial and are not forthcoming. The bailiffs of Canterbury have nothing to show in excuse of their failure to produce them. "Therefore there must be judgment of them for escape of the aforesaid prisoners." That is the way the Eyre worked. That is the way in which, to quote Matthew Paris again, the Justices filled the King's coffers. I will give you another instance dealing with the escape of a prisoner, and I am choosing it because it notes incidentally the somewhat strange conditions of the tenure by which certain people held their land. It was presented that a woman who had been sentenced to be hanged had escaped from the custody of the bailiff of the liberty of Middleton in Kent. The bailiff was brought before the Justices to make what explanation he could. He pleaded that he had handed over the woman for execution to six men of the liberty who held their lands on condition that they executed judgment on condemned prisoners. But this plea availed him naught with the Justices. Both he and the whole liberty were put under judgment. Escaping prisoners provided the King with much revenue. One last example of this from the presentments of a dozen. A man was arrested for larceny and put into prison, and he broke out therefrom. So the keeper of the prison is under judgment. But this prisoner, as soon as he had escaped from prison, took sanctuary in a church. It was the duty of the whole township to see that he did not escape from the church. But he did escape; and the whole township consequently came under judgment. And so, the record concludes, there are two escapes by one prisoner. And a penalty has to be paid for each of them.

A presentment might involve merely a failure to perform a duty, a duty to repair a bridge or a road; and in such a case the Justices would make further inquiries of the dozen and then make such order for the immediate repair of the bridge or road and the amercement of the defaulter as seemed good to them; or there might be something more in such a case than mere neglect. It was presented that a certain man had allowed his fences to remain broken that the cattle of his neighbours might stray on to his land, whereupon he impounded them and extorted money from their owners for letting them have them back. "For this let him be grievously punished," was the sentence of the Justices.

Let me now give you an illustration from the Nottinghamshire Eyre of 4 Edward III of the iniquitous way in which these Pleas of the Crown were worked for the pecuniary advantage of the King. One of the dozens presented at that Eyre the following facts. A thief had stolen and driven off thirty sheep from their owner's land. The owner quickly discovered the theft and pursued the thief, who, finding himself in imminent peril of being captured, abandoned the sheep and took sanctuary in the nearest church, where, you will remember, he was safe from arrest, and there he was allowed—indeed, he could not be prevented—to abjure the realm and depart in peace to the port assigned to him for his departure from England. The Sheriff, guided by elementary common sense, in his lamentable ignorance of the law, naturally restored the sheep to their owner. What happened when the dozen made this presentment of facts in answer to one of the Articles of the Eyre? The presiding Justice at once exclaimed, apparently with some show of heat, that the owner was most certainly not entitled to have his sheep back. They had been stolen, and he had not prosecuted the thief to conviction. What chance had he of doing so? Before the thief could be arrested he had taken sanctuary. He certainly could not be arrested while he was in the church. Then he abjured the realm with the accustomed formalities, and was necessarily allowed to take his way to the coast; and again no one might touch him. But according to strict law a man whose property had been stolen must prove by bringing about the actual conviction of the thief that it had in fact been stolen from him, before he could obtain restitution of it. The working of the law of the land regarding the right of sanctuary and abjuration of the realm had debarred the unfortunate owner of the sheep from making the smallest attempt to prosecute the thief. And because he had not done what the law made it impossible for him to do Herle, who was sitting as Chief Justice of the Eyre, hotly exclaimed that of course he was not entitled to the return of the sheep. The Sheriff had no business to give them to him. They had become the King's property, and the Sheriff would be held responsible by the Court for seeing that the King got them, or got their full value. It was not often that the mediaeval reporters ventured to slip a word of criticism into their reports, but he who took down this story well over 600 years ago for our learning to-day felt constrained to add a word or two of his own. "A strange thing it seems," he wrote, "that the owner was not to have them back, for no shadow of fault could be found in him." And yet there was really nothing uncommon in the facts. Whenever property of any sort was stolen and the thief abandoned it to avoid arrest and managed to escape, then, when these facts were presented at the next Eyre the Justices would certainly rule that the stolen property, whatever it might be, was forfeit to the King, and they would straightway order that he should have it or its value; and someone was made personally responsible for seeing that he did have it.

Let me now tell you a story from the reports of the Pleas of the Crown of the London Eyre of 1321, a story with an unwonted touch of comedy about it. There is little, very little, but grim harshness and severity revealed by a study of the Pleas of the Crown as a whole.

In the London Eyre of 1321 a presentment was made against John of Crombwelle, Constable of the Tower, also Chamberlain to the King and a Peer of Parliament, that he had wrongfully seized a coasting vessel, laden with tiles, and also a boat, and had appropriated them to his own use. Some other charges of like irregularities were made against him. He made what defence of himself he could before the Justices, who ordered him to come up before them on a future day for judgment. But he seems to have been saved the trouble of appearing again— though I do not quite see why he should have been—for the Roll of the Eyre records that the aforesaid John of Crombwelle did not appear on that day because he had been removed from the Constableship of the Tower by reason of his neglect to repair the living-rooms in the Tower, whereby rain had come in upon the bed of the Queen of England while giving birth there to a daughter, that Princess Joan of the Tower who subsequently became the wife of David II, King of Scotland, the prisoner for eleven long years of his wife's brother, Edward III of England. The birth of the Princess happened very awkwardly not only for the negligent John of Crombwelle but for the general arrangements of the Eyre. I suppose that some reasonable degree of quietness was considered necessary for the Queen in the circumstances, a degree of quietness which was not possible with all the turmoil of the Eyre going on inside the Tower; and so the Justices were turned out of the Tower itself, and accommodation had to be found for those of them who were taking the Common Pleas in a wooden house in the second ward of the Tower, while the Justices hearing the Pleas of the Crown sat in a small house adjoining it. But the Queen's condition was not the only reason assigned for this removal of the Justices. There was also another reason, one which I am afraid would not make her bedroom in the Tower any the more comfortable for the Queen. The Earl of Hereford and his supporters were in open insurrection on every side of London, and it was necessary to take steps for strengthening the fortifications of the Tower, and this could not be conveniently done while the courts of the Eyre were sitting inside it. It is interesting to note that this insurrection brought some advantage and comfort to the citizens of London. When the Justices rose for the Easter vacation the chronicler's wailing note is that the Eyre had then gone on for nine weeks in tribulation and bitter straits. But when the Justices resume their sittings there is a great change. No longer do they show the same cruelty as before; for whereas up to Easter they had been like lions ever ready to spring at their prey, now they became more

like lambs, and the reason for this welcome change was
that Humphrey de Bohun, Earl of Hereford and Essex,
and his supporters, had just risen most unexpectedly in
Wales, and, by their harrying and outrages there had
aroused an alarm throughout all England until then un-
heard of in our times. It had come home to the King
and his Justices of the Eyre that something more than
the material fortification of his capital city was necessary;
and that disaffection amongst the citizens had better not
be encouraged by the savagery of Courts supposed to be
administering justice.

Many presentments by the dozens involved a charge
of felony against some one who was not in custody. In
these cases the Justices ordered the arrest of the person
involved. When the presentment was formally made by
the dozen, the Court turned to the prisoner and asked
him what he had to say. If he said, as he almost certainly
would say, that he was not guilty of the charge brought
against him, they then asked him how he desired to
acquit himself; and the accused man would say that he
put himself on a jury; and by a jury he was at once tried.
And that raises a question for us to-day which is not very
easily answered; which cannot be answered at all except
in a good many words, and even then not with certainty.
By what jury was such a man tried? By the presenting
dozen, or by some other jury? At first sight it would
seem unfair that the accusers should also be the judges.
But the presenting jury, the dozen, did not in the first
instance make their presentments as matters of proven
fact. They were relying in much of what they presented
on hearsay, on recollections which they were not themselves able at the moment to confirm. And therefore
their presentment was far from being the same thing as

a verdict given upon oath after hearing evidence; and they might not improperly have this further duty cast upon them. But had they? If the only evidence on the point we had was one of the manuscript year books of the Kent Eyre of 1313 we might feel no doubt. According to that manuscript "if a dozen make a presentment against anyone under any Article of the Eyre, the Sheriff shall bring up such person, and when he comes he shall put himself upon the jury that indicted him." But the reports of the Eyres make it impossible for us to accept this statement as accurately setting forth the actual practice in all cases. That the presenting jury often did form the trying jury seems certain. That it always formed a part of the trying jury seems all but certain. We must remember that there were only twelve jurors present from each hundred; and so, as we cannot well suppose a jury of fewer than twelve, there was no alternative jury of any hundred. And we are told sometimes that when a jury, after hearing evidence, has returned a verdict of not guilty the whole twelve of them are put under judgment and amerced for having contradicted their original presentment. And here I may remark that the troubles of a dozen who, as a trying jury, acquitted some one against whom they, as the presenting dozen, had made a presentment, did not end by being put under judgment and fined, but they had to find out who really was the guilty person. "You are not going to get off so lightly as this," Chief Justice Scrope said to a dozen at the Eyre of Northamptonshire of 3 Edward III who had found a verdict of not guilty in favour of one against whom they had previously made a presentment of robbery. "We are certainly of opinion that a robbery was committed. You will now tell us who actually committed it." And he sent the dozen away to find out. And I am sure that unpleasant things happened to them if they did not, or if they made another unfortunate guess. Some one had got to be convicted of that robbery. And the sooner the dozen convicted somebody of it, and somebody's lands and chattels became forfeited to the King, the better for the dozen at any rate. It is conceivable that their second or third verdicts about that robbery might not be so conscientiously formulated as their first one.

It is certain that sometimes the presenting dozen formed only a part of the trying jury, but where they did not form the whole of it they always seem to form part of it, when we have any information at all as to its composition. An accused man desired to be tried by a jury of the hundred where he was born. The Court told him that he ought to be tried by the jury of the hundred in which it was alleged that the offence was committed, that is by the presenting jury; but allowed him, as a sort of compromise, to be tried by the combined juries of both hundreds. I have not time to go fully into this matter now, but I think that I am justified in saying that all the evidence we have at present points to the conclusion that the constitution of a trying jury was wholly in the discretion of the Court, with the one condition that the jurors of the presenting hundred must form part of it; and that the number of the trying jury was not limited to twelve.

Lecture III

I HOPE that I have made it plain to you what a terrible
engine of oppression and extortion the Pleas of the
Crown, as embodied in the Articles of the Eyre, were
capable of becoming, and did, as a matter of fact, become.
It was the commission to hold these Pleas of the Crown,
with its unlimited powers of imprisonment and amercement, which set the General Eyre in its unholy eminence,
which made it a thing apart from all other judicial
commissions of the middle ages, which made it a terror
and an abomination in the sight of all men. Imprisonment
was scarcely ever inflicted by the Justices hearing the
Pleas of the Crown as a punishment in itself, but merely
to force those upon whom it was inflicted to purchase
their restoration to liberty by the payment of a fine to
the King. The Justices of the General Eyre did many
other things besides holding these Pleas of the Crown.
They heard and determined assizes and actions of all
sorts. But as their procedure in these differed not at all
from the procedure of the Court of Common Bench at
Westminster in the same matters, I need say nothing
about it in the lectures in which I am dealing with the
special characteristics of the Eyre itself. Another of the
powers of the Justices of the Eyre was to hold a Gaol
Delivery. Here again their procedure was the same as
that of justices who were commissioned from time to
time to deliver the gaols, and held no other commission.
But here it is necessary to say something further. The
Justices holding the Pleas of the Crown were trying

charges of felony plentifully. The Justices delivering the
gaols were doing the same thing. What was the difference
between them? The Justices trying the Crown Pleas were
trying, you will remember, persons against whom presentments involving charges of felony had been made by
the dozens. These people were all enjoying full liberty;
and the first step taken by the Justices on the presentment
by a dozen of a charge of felony was to order the arrest
of the person charged. The dozens were going to take no
risks. To a great extent they were acting on hearsay.
They knew, or had heard, that such or such a crime had
been committed, perhaps several years ago, and that the
name of this person or that was connected with it, that
he had perhaps been arrested for it. They had no certain
knowledge of what had happened afterwards; or, if even
they had, they thought it wiser to ignore it. A crime had
at some time or other been committed within their
hundred, and somebody had come under suspicion in
connexion with it. So much they knew, and so much
they said. And the Justices straightway ordered the
arrest of the person implicated; and that person if he
could be found, was immediately arrested and brought
before the Justices and put upon his trial. Just consider
the circumstances for a moment. Was it likely that
anyone, knowing what happened at these General Eyres,
knowing the haphazard, wholesale ways in which the
dozens, for their own protection, made presentments,
racking their memories for any crimes or rumours of
crimes which had been committed within their jurisdiction for years past, and knowing also that there was a
reasonable probability of his being found guilty and
promptly hanged, would quietly continue in his own
neighbourhood and wait there till the Justices came and

ordered his arrest. Of course it was not? And when these men are arrested and put upon their trial we may feel quite sure that one of three things is going to happen. They will have such a clear defence on the facts as will make their acquittal quite sure, or they will be able to prove from the rolls of some gaol delivery that they have been previously tried on the same charge and have been acquitted, or they will have the King's pardon in their pocket. I do not think that there were more than two or three men hanged by the Justices hearing Crown Pleas at the Kent Eyre of 1313, and these were taken red-handed for crimes committed during the actual session of the Eyre and had no opportunity of escaping. And it was the same at all other Eyres. But when the Justices turned their attention to trying prisoners already in custody, to delivering the gaols, there is a very different story to be told. These men, to use a modern expression, had been committed for trial by the county courts and other local courts having initial criminal jurisdiction, and were kept in gaol, unless they escaped, as a great many of them did, until a commission of Gaol Delivery or a General Eyre came along and tried them. By the Justices delivering gaols a goodly amount of hanging was done. Men, and women too, were hanged upon very small provocation in those days. Listen to this statement of the law by the Justices sitting at Canterbury. "If presentment be made that one is suspected of theft to the value of ten pence or less, he is to be arrested; and if of this he be convicted he shall go to prison at the discretion of the Justices; and if afterwards he be convicted of stealing to the further value of two pence more or less, so that the whole value amount to twelve pence halfpenny, he shall have judgment of life and limb."

Again: "If two or three jointly steal goods to the value of twelve pence halfpenny they shall all have judgment of life and limb." Yes, there was much hanging done by the Justices at a gaol delivery. The Justices of the Eyre were commissioned to hold Pleas of the Crown and they were also commissioned to deliver the gaols. Let us try to distinguish shortly what they did in this double capacity. The Crown Pleas division of the Eyre was in fact, whatever it might be in theory, a travelling branch of the Exchequer, with enormous powers of levying money by fines and amercements. It was little, not primarily, concerned with the administration of justice. It was the business of Gaol Deliveries to deliver gaols and to hang such prisoners as had neither been able to escape—to the subsequent profit, by the way, of the King—nor to show conclusively that they ought never to have been arrested. It was the business of the Justices hearing Crown Pleas to see that every fact in connexion with every criminal trial, either before themselves or at any previous gaol delivery, that might possibly furnish a reason why somebody should be amerced or somebody's goods confiscated was brought to their notice, and that that amercement was got into the King's coffers and that those goods were confiscated to the King's profit. A man, for example, was hanged at some previous gaol delivery. Possibly he was possessed of chattels. If he were, of course these are forfeit to the King; and it is for the Justices holding the Crown Pleas to see not only that they were confiscated, but that their value was rightly assessed, for it was the assessed value of them for which the Sheriff was responsible. The King did not want to be troubled with a miscellaneous assortment of all kinds of odds and ends. It was their money value which he wanted, and it was their money value that it was the business of the Justices to see that he got. All sorts of people who ought to have come forward at one stage or another of the proceedings in connexion with the crime did not come forward. Of course they have thereby become liable to be amerced, and the Justices take care to see that they are amerced and that they pay their amercements or stay in prison until they do. But another lot of people were their sureties for attendance, and so these, too, must be amerced. Almost any folio in our old manuscript Year Books of the proceedings in Eyre of the Crown Pleas division will show that that division existed to fill the King's coffers and not to maintain the King's peace. But there is so much else to be said about other matters that I must say no more now about either the Crown Pleas or the Gaol Delivery. Yet I hope that I have said enough to make you realize something of what these Crown Pleas meant, to understand and to sympathize with the fear and dread with which they darkened and troubled the minds and lives of our mediaeval ancestors.

Another very important branch of the business done at an Eyre was that done in virtue of the commission empowering the Justices to try writs of *quo warranto*. In speaking of the manorial courts I reminded you that under the feudal system introduced by William I the mere possession of land or of tenants entitled the lord of the manor to hold a court for enforcing the custom of the manor. It was recognized that jurisdiction was involved in this mere fact of possession and followed from it. But this inherent jurisdiction did not entitle the manorial lords to do more than administer justice to their tenants in small disputes amongst themselves, to punish breaches of the custom of the manor. This was all the power which the King had granted to them. He had not, by granting a manor, granted along with it any of those powers which were known as regalities, powers which could not be exercised by any but the Sovereign himself, unless it were by virtue of a special charter from the Sovereign conferring these powers on the subject in whose favour such charter was granted. The earlier Kings granted many such charters. Many of the greater manorial lords were exercising, and exercising rightly and legally, royal powers. They had, many of them, the right to try felons in their own manorial courts and to hang them if they were convicted and to confiscate their possessions to their own advantage. They had the right to hold a view of frankpledge; they had a right to deal with infractions of the assize of bread and beer, and to put all penalties inflicted for such infractions into their own pockets. They had a right, some of them, to be free from all murder fines. They could of their own authority institute markets and fairs, receiving for their own use all the accruing profits. They could do, one or other of them, a hundred things which naturally only the King himself could do. Some of the greater lords had acquired even greater powers than those I have named. The Archbishops of York, for instance, had the right of maintaining three mints for the coining of their own money. The Abbot of Battle, and he was not alone in his privilege, had the right of making the Justices of the Eyre come to his manor of Wye and there hold what we may call an Eyre within an Eyre. Nothing touching his own people might be dealt with at Canterbury by the Justices appointed by the King. One or more of them must come to Wye and there join themselves with the Abbot, who within his own jurisdiction had the full powers of a

Justice in Eyre, and there, and there only, deal with all matters arising within his liberty. This minor Eyre was in every way independent of and separate from the greater Eyre of the rest of the county. It even had its own independent set of plea rolls; and you may see them to this day, as things apart, in the Public Record Office. And who shall try to put a limit to the powers of the Prince Bishops of Durham or the Earls Palatine of Chester? These seem to have had within their respective jurisdictions the full power of the Sovereign himself. The King's supremacy over all persons and in all causes within his dominions was not the theory of those days. Though many of the manorial lords were exercising their royal functions rightly enough, by virtue of the King's special grant of them, yet, as time went on, other lords gradually began to arrogate to themselves, without any warrant at all, the right of doing like things. They began to assume a right to punish breaches of the peace or of the assize of bread and beer, and to take for their own profit the amercements arising therefrom. They held a remunerative view of frankpledge; and, one and another of them, when Edward I came to the throne, were usurping royal powers to their own pecuniary profit, and consequently to the pecuniary loss of the King, without any right to do so. This was a growing abuse which began seriously to exercise the minds of the King's advisers. This money which these manorial lords were illicitly putting into their own pockets must somehow be got to its rightful destination, which was undoubtedly the King's pocket. How was it to be done? In the beginning it was done in this way. The King ordered the courts of the different hundreds to make a return to him of the manorial lords within their several jurisdictions who were exercising any powers outside those inherent in the possession of a manor. When he got these returns made, he sent to each of the lords named in them what was called a writ of *quo warranto*, a writ calling upon them to say by what warrant they claimed to exercise this or that royal power. And then he sent judicial commissions throughout the country to hear what the manorial lords implicated had to say, and to adjudicate upon their claims. I imagine that a great deal of unpleasantness ensued. The King's Serjeants, officially opposing the claims of the lords, were at first inclined to take a very high position. To have adopted their contentions would have meant depriving many lords of manors of powers which they had been exercising without objection from a time beyond memory, for the right to exercise which they could plead nothing but immemorial prescription. If they had ever had any charter of grant at all it had long been lost. To have declared that all these privileges had been illegally assumed and must no longer be used, as the King's Serjeants contended, would have created a great uproar in the country; and those were not days when the King cared to alienate lightly the sympathy and loyalty of his more important subjects. The consequence was that actual judgments were scarcely ever given by the Justices. The matter was adjourned for judgment at Westminster, and as a rule no judgment was ever given. Then by the statutes passed at Gloucester in the 18th year of Edward I it was allowed that uninterrupted possession of these royal rights, these regalities, since the accession of Richard I, roughly a period of a hundred years, should be taken to give a valid and incontestible right to them. And that, by the way, is the origin of the theory which still prevails that the beginning of legal memory is the first year of Richard I. Though the issue of these early writs of *quo warranto* was in one way a failure, in another way it was successful. Silent usurpation of regalities was no longer possible. Any lord who could not show a hundred years' uninterrupted possession of them would quickly be deprived of them, and punished for usurping them. These statutes of 18 Edward I brought about an important change in respect of the trial of the writs of *quo warranto*, a change which, telling the story of the Eyres, I must note here. "Also our lord the King hath granted that for sparing of the costs and expenses of the people of this realm, pleas of *Quo warranto* shall henceforth be heard in the Eyres." And so for the future no Justices in Eyre went out without a commission to hold these pleas. What was their procedure? In the common summons of the Eyre all those who claimed to be in possession of any regalities either by right of a royal grant or in any other way were bidden to attend on the first day of the Eyre and then and there make their claims. If they failed to do this they were liable to lose all their privileges. Some of them did fail to make their claims, in which case they ran some risk of forfeiting their rights, and probably had to pay some fine to the King for being allowed subsequently to make their claim. When these claims had been entered a writ of *quo warranto* was served upon each claimant, and he had to appear before the Justices and make out what case he could for himself. Sometimes a claimant upon whom such a writ had been served failed to appear to answer it, and so created further difficulties for himself. At the Eyre of Kent of 1313, for instance, John of Lenham was summoned to answer the King by what warrant he claimed to have free warren in his demesne

lands and to hold a market on every Tuesday. John
failed to appear, and thereupon the King's Serjeant
prayed that the franchise might be seized into the King's
hand, that is re-assumed by the power which had granted
it. And thereupon the Sheriff was ordered by the Court
to seize the franchise straightway into the King's hand,
and to be responsible to the King for the profits, and to
have a man at the market to collect the tolls and other
profits of the market for the King. "And now," added
the Chief Justice, "let John sue as soon as he likes, for
unless he replevies these franchises within this Eyre he
will lose them for ever"; that is, unless, on some payment
to the King, he is allowed to regain the position of one
who has made his claim at the right time and so have
an opportunity of substantiating it, he will lose his
privileges, whatever right he may have to them. Then
what happens is something like this. When John's counsel
appears to make John's claim, the Chief Justice tells him
that any rights John may possibly have had have been
resumed by the King. Then John's Serjeant prays that
John may be allowed to replevy them, that is to put
himself in the same position to argue his case as he would
have been if he had not neglected to appear when he
ought to have appeared. "Willingly," says the Chief
Justice, "but you will pay a fine to the King"; and when
John has done this to the satisfaction of the Court, he
is allowed to say what he can for himself in substantiation
of his claim. I may tell you that this particular claimant
proved that he was entitled to the privileges he claimed
by a charter of Edward II himself, which could not have
been more than six years old; and so he was confirmed
in the possession of them, at any rate till the next Eyre.
There was one undoubted advantage in hearing these

pleas of *quo warranto* at the Eyre. They were settled there and then. There was no adjournment to Westminster, with the strong probability of no judgment at all being given. These claims had to be renewed at every Eyre, but when they were once allowed a record to this effect was entered on the roll of the Eyre, and at the following Eyre a claimant had only to vouch this record in support of the claim, and it was thereupon allowed. Let me conclude this section of my lecture by repeating to you some rather shrewd remarks made by Justice Spigurnel. A certain Abbot had claimed the privilege of having what was called a free warren, that is of maintaining a place for breeding and keeping for his own profit, hares and rabbits, pheasants and partridges and the like. The Abbot had failed to make his claim at the right time, and in course of the consequent discussion Spigurnel said: "If I were King I would grant warren readily enough; for, to begin with, the King gets eleven marks and a half for the grant. Then he gets a fine of ten pounds for breach of warren from anyone who hunts in another man's warren; and if the lord of the warren accept compensation from anybody who has hunted in his warren without his permission he will forfeit his warren; and he will have to pay a fine to the King for having taken to his own profit what really belonged to the King, for every charter of warren granted by the King recites that all penalties belong to the King; and so the King gets all the profit, except that the lord may amuse himself by hunting whenever he likes and may sell what he kills in his warren at the prices allowed by the assize of food, that is three halfpence for a hare, four pence for a rabbit, and so on for the other beasts of the chase."

One of the most important and interesting characteristics of the Eyre was the power of the Justices to hear
and determine all matters of complaint by what was
known as a bill instead of in the ordinary way by writ,
which was the only procedure open to the Justices sitting
in the Courts at Westminster. In the lectures on the
Year Books which I gave in this University last summer
I spoke at some length on the nature of these bills. As
those lectures have been printed[1] I need not repeat what
I then said. It will be sufficient to say that now the
King's Justices in Eyre had, speaking generally, the powers
of the King himself. They represented the King in a very
special and full sense. The King's residual or extra-
ordinary function of causing justice to be done where
ordinary means failed lay in their hands, and they were
not only entitled but bound to exercise it. In the ordinary
way a complainant before the King's Justices had to
begin by getting a suitable writ from the Chancery in
London, and this writ had to be worded in the most
scrupulously careful way. It could not be subsequently
amended in form, and the smallest error, even a gram-
matical error in the Latin in which it was written, might
be fatal to the plaintiff's case when it came before the
Court. A bill in Eyre might be written by anyone; and
some of them, many of them, were certainly written by
people without any legal training, by people whose general
illiteracy is patent not only in their hand-writing but in
the uncouthness of their language and their amazing
disregard of the ordinary rules of grammar. These bills
were an appeal over the head of the law to the paternal
powers, so to speak, of the King as father of his people,
put where he was, to quote Bracton again, to serve as

[1] *The Year Books* (Cambridge University Press).

God's Vicar on earth, to judge between right and wrong, to see that all his subjects bore themselves uprightly and honestly, that none harmeth another, that every man kept unimpaired what was rightly his. They were usually, almost always, written in the Anglo-Norman of the time; many of them in Anglo-Norman of a peculiarly illiterate kind. Some very few of them are in Latin. I have seen none in English. A writ could not be altered or amended. These bills might be freely altered or amended if it were found, when they came before the court, that they did not correctly or clearly set forth the complainant's case. Slips that would have been immediately fatal in a writ were put straight in a bill without any detriment to the complainant. In many cases, too, a remedy for wrong suffered could be got by means of a bill before the Justices of Eyre where no remedy at all could be got by a writ, a fact which is stated more than once or twice in the reports in our old manuscripts. There was no writ to meet the case. A bill would meet any case where hardship or wrong had been suffered. Restrictive injunctions might be obtained by bill, or orders for the performance of some duty which had not been performed. The Justices inquired into complaints brought by bill in a very thoroughgoing way. They were bound by none of the ordinary rules of law or procedure. They even interrogated the parties, a thing unknown to common law process. In Eyre alone was access to the King's plenary power possible to his subjects. As yet it is only to his Justices of the Eyre that the King has lent so much of his *persona* as will enable them to do abstract justice in the failure of, or in spite of, common law and statute law. Hereafter the same power will accrue to the King's Justices sitting at Westminster, and later yet will be withdrawn from these to become the special and characteristic appanage of the Court of Chancery and the warrant for its equitable jurisdiction.

These bills, of which many are still preserved in the Public Record Office, are extremely valuable for the light which they throw upon the conditions of social life in provincial England in the thirteenth and fourteenth centuries. Many of them are really in the form of narratives of events, and no other documents of which I have any knowledge present us with such varied and complete pictures of what happened, of what people did and how they acted in those far-off years. Perhaps the first characteristic of the times that strikes us on studying these old bills is the complete absence of anything like what we may call police protection. The weak seem to be entirely at the mercy of the strong. Not even a neighbour cares to interfere to help a neighbour in danger of loss of property or of life or limb. Here is an example of this, gathered from one of these old bills that came before the Justices of the Staffordshire Eyre of 1293, being the 21st year of Edward I. Iseult Edrich had recovered possession by due process of law of a house and land from the wife of William of Bywood, who also was called Iseult. Whatever grievance William and his wife may have considered they had, Iseult Edrich was undoubtedly in legal possession of the house. She was living in it, and on the Saturday that was St Valentine's Day in 1293 William Bywood and his wife came to it and claimed to have possession of it. Iseult naturally refused them admission. Now in the adjoining house one Adam the chapman or pedlar lived. When Iseult refused to let William Bywood and his wife come into her house, William sounded a blast on a horn and his wife forced her way into Adam's house—Adam, I suppose, was not on his guard—broke through the flimsy lath and plaster party-wall which separated the entrances of the two houses and pulled back the inside bolt of Iseult's door. Then she flung open the door, rushed inside the house, seized Iseult by the neck and all but strangled her, and finally drove her out of the house. And all the time a small crowd of neighbours—we have the names of seven men amongst them—were looking on, making not the smallest attempt, apparently, to protect Iseult from the murderous attack that was being made on her. If these bills give us anything like a true picture of the people of those times, then they seem to show that one of their most remarkable characteristics was the callous stolidity with which they stood by and watched man, woman or child struggling against odds, in dire peril of life or limb, without being prompted to render the least assistance.

Let me now tell you a story about another Iseult, illustrative of provincial life at the time. This Iseult was, I suppose, a lady of some social importance in her own neighbourhood. She was the wife of the lord of the manor of Burton-on-Trent, and was quite possibly looked upon by her less highly placed lady friends as a model of the social proprieties, to be copied as nearly as might be by themselves. One day early in May in 1292 this lady went to the house of one Margery, and there, for no reason that is assigned, attacked Margery, felled her to the ground, and, while she lay there bleeding and half dead, battered her head with stones, thereby entirely destroying the hearing of her left ear. And the story as it is told on behalf of Margery ends this way: "And this wrong is known of many, for the said Margery was carried in a cart to the county court that the wrong done to her might be seen, and because her life was despaired of." This is an interesting early example of the perpetuation of evidence; but a ride in a springless cart over jolting roads scarcely seems the happiest prescription for one in Margery's condition. The whole story gives us a lively picture of the possibilities of a thirteenth century Staffordshire drawing-room if anything should happen to annoy the lady of the house.

Here is another gruesome story—I am afraid that I can give you no very cheerful ones from these old bills in Eyre—of just about the same date and of events happening in that same county. There was an old woman, Margery by name, living in Codsall in a house which she held as part of her dower. When she fell sick her daughter Alice, who I suppose had married and gone to a home of her own, came to stay with her mother that she might nurse her. Alice was, at any rate it is part of her story that she was, entitled, as heiress, upon her mother's death, to the dower house in which her mother was living. Margery dies, and the breath is no sooner out of her body than a rough crew break into the house and seize everything therein on which they can lay their hands. They assault Alice and turn her and every one with her, including Margery's executors, out of the house, and the old woman's body is left lying there "unburied, abandoned and forsaken," and there it was apparently still lying when Alice embodied her story in the bill which may be read to-day in the Public Record Office. I could go on multiplying stories like these, but there would be no purpose in doing so when so much else remains to be said. But ever and always these poor women are left to fight their battles alone. No one interferes, apparently, neither constable nor neighbour.

Let us turn to another class of stories throwing some light on the social conditions of the time. When a man wanted to make some provision for his old age, for the days when he should no longer be able to earn his own living by manual labour, what did he do? There were no insurance companies with which he could negotiate for an annuity. The only means open to him was to covenant with some other man that this latter should, for a certain consideration in money and goods, and perhaps in some bit of land, provide him with board and lodging for the rest of his life. Agreements of this kind seem to have been not at all uncommon, but the security for their being observed was woefully small. At best it depended upon the continued ability of the obligees to keep them. Even if such an one continued well able to keep his covenant, he might, and we see from these old bills that he not infrequently did, refuse to do so; and before legal remedy could be got, if it could be got at all, the defrauded annuitant—if one may so call him—might be reduced to absolute beggary in his old age. And I will ask you to note here and appreciate the full meaning of the fact that practically the only remedy that was open to one who had been so defrauded was by a bill in Eyre, and Eyres came round at the oftenest only once in seven years. So for full seven years such an one might be left to starve and beg and more likely than not die of hunger and exposure before he had even the chance of getting any remedy. Perhaps the usual practice in agreements of this kind was for the insurer to take his pensioner into his own house and there give him food and lodging. But this, some of our old bills show us, was clearly a case of the spider inviting the fly into his parlour, or something very like it. We get glimpses of cases where horrible

barbarity seems to have been practised. I have one
particularly pathetic case in my mind. It is a story
couched in such illiterate language that we cannot be sure
that we wholly understand it. For the sake of clearness
of narration let us call the pensioner John, the man with
whom he made his agreement Richard. At some time
towards the end of the thirteenth century John paid
Richard six marks—a mark, you will remember was the
equivalent of thirteen shillings and four pence, and money
in the thirteenth century had a very much larger purchasing value than it has to-day—and in consideration of
this sum of six marks Richard covenanted in writing to
provide John with board and lodging. As soon as Richard
got possession of John's money he seems to have taken
him into his own house and kept him in close confinement
there, in some sort of cellar or outhouse, chained to the
floor or wall, doling out to him just enough bread to keep
him alive. John was lucky enough to make his escape
somehow and to get his complaint brought before the
Justices in Eyre. And there, I am glad to be able to tell
you, he seems to have got some sort of satisfaction.
Richard was obliged to admit that he had been in fault,
and the Court allowed him to come to a settlement with
John. I cannot tell you what the terms of that settlement were, but as John accepted them, and as they were
apparently sanctioned by the Court, I suppose that they
were reasonably satisfactory to John. But John was in the
end one of the more lucky ones. How many were there who
made the like agreements and then received the same
barbarous treatment and did not escape to tell their tale?

These stories which I have been telling you are true
stories of real people who lived in that England of long
ago which our writers of romance call Merry England.

They are not figments. I could show you in proof of every incident of which I have told you the actual documents which were written centuries ago from the information given by the injured people, documents quite possibly seen and handled by them. And the stories I have told you are merely sample stories, picked out here and there from the many which have come down to us; and for every one that has come down to us, I suppose that hundreds—I speak advisedly—have perished. It is a distressing fact that of all the countless bills which must have been presented at the very many Eyres held in England from Henry II's time to Edward III's only those which are presented at three Eyres of Edward I and at one of Edward III, and probably not nearly all even of them, have, so far as I know, survived. By what lucky accident these have been preserved I suppose no one can say; but as so few out of so many have come down to us it seems probable that the practice was to destroy all the bills at the conclusion of an Eyre. But it is a very grievous loss.

I must not spend all my available time in reviving stories of oppression and inhumanity. These old bills have much else of interest to disclose to us, much which throws light on the working of mediaeval provincial life, on the conditions under which it was lived. Though such a lamentable number of them have perished, yet many still remain; and until these have been carefully read and studied no adequate history of English social life in the middle ages can be written.

Some of you will remember a picture in *Punch* of now a good many years ago, the under-written legend of which still gets itself quoted every now and again. A stranger has ventured into the street of a mining village. "Who's

that, Bill?" "I dunno." "Then let's 'eave a brick at
'im." That picture and legend came into my mind when
I read one of these old bills which seemed to make it
plain that if a man ventured out of his own district he
ran, and knew that he ran, some risk of rough usage.
One William who lived in Hereford in Edward I's time
had his horse stolen, and he set out in search of it. But
before doing so, he, prudent man, knowing the customs
of his time, thought it necessary to provide himself with
a certificate from the community of the town of Hereford,
formally sealed with their common seal, declaring that
he was an honest man out on the honest business of
looking for his own horse. But even this did not save
him when he got to Marchamley in the next county of
Shropshire. As he was entering this place he was attacked
by one John Cock who assaulted him with great violence
and even stole from him his certificate of respectability
from the authorities of Hereford, and then drove him
out of the town. This happened on the Saturday next
before the Feast of the Ascension in the fourteenth year
of the reign of Edward I. It was not till six years later
that the Justices of the Eyre came into Shropshire; and
it was consequently not till six years after the assault
was made upon him that William could make his complaint. No wonder that these complaints seem so often
to have failed. How, in most cases, could a man prove
his case after an interval of five or six or even more
years?

Now I will tell you the story, so far as I can, of a
mediaeval financial transaction which shows that even at
the time when the taking of any interest at all for a loan
of money was forbidden, a very considerable interest was
exacted, a percentage which does not look small even

when compared with the interest which modern money-lenders are said to charge sometimes. Somewhere about the year 1272 Thomas Trie of Ludlow had need of twenty shillings. None of his friends would oblige him, and so he went to the Jews. He found a Jew in Bridgnorth who was willing to lend him the twenty shillings he wanted, but only upon the condition that Hugh Donvile, who was bailiff and constable of Bridgnorth, would guarantee the repayment of the loan. If this guarantee were given then the Jew said that he would lend Thomas twenty shillings from the Feast of St Lawrence to the Feast of St Michael —it strikes one as a little odd to find this Jew making his computations by this Christian chronology—that is to say from August 10 to September 29, a period of seven weeks, for a repayment of thirty shillings. This means annual interest at the rate of just about 375 per cent. Thomas then went off to Hugh the bailiff to try to persuade him to become his guarantor. But Hugh was difficult of persuasion. In the end he promised to guarantee the payment of the thirty shillings at the stated time if Thomas would put him in possession of a certain house. Thomas did this, and then went back to the Jew with Hugh's guarantee, and the Jew thereupon handed seven shillings to Thomas by way of an instalment, but Thomas never got anything more from him than those seven shillings, though the Jew kept Hugh's bond for the repayment of thirty. In due course the Jew goes to Hugh with the bond and claims the thirty shillings. Hugh bargains with him and manages to get his bond returned to him on the payment of fifteen shillings, although Thomas had never received more than seven. Thomas now proposes to redeem the house of which he had given Hugh possession by a payment to Hugh of the fifteen shillings which Hugh had paid to the Jew to recover his bond. But Hugh wants his commission. He refuses to give up the house for less than twenty-four shillings. Thomas does not want to lose his house if he can help it, so he contrives to borrow twenty-four shillings somehow and somewhere, and pays them over to Hugh. "But never since," so the bill concludes, "hath that Thomas been able to get entrance into the house nor to recover his money; and Hugh detaineth it to the grievous damage of the same Thomas. And Thomas prayeth for God's sake that the truth of this matter may be inquired of by a good jury; and of this he prayeth remedy for God's sake." All this happened about 1272. The Eyre at which Thomas made his complaint was just about twenty years later. Whether from lack of evidence after so many years, or from some other cause, the matter seems to have gone no further than the summoning of Hugh to appear to answer and the taking of sureties for his appearance. Something or other happened which caused Thomas to drop the prosecution of his complaint. And when a complainant was fighting down in Staffordshire in 1293 a man like Hugh Donvile one can understand that a good many things might happen, for we know from other sources that Hugh was an official of great power and influence, who largely used his influence in oppressing "faithful subjects and harmless men for the sake of lucre"; and not only did he oppress the innocent but he was always open to a bribe to allow the guilty to escape. And that is the end of Thomas's story. I know nowhere else than in these old bills where you will find the like stories of quite obscure people, yet of people characteristic of their own class and that by far the largest class of people then living in England, told with such fulness of detail and in such plain and natural language. These bills, by far the most of them at any rate, were not written by lawyers in legal language, but by anyone who could put even the most unskilled pen to parchment and tell his story in the crudest fashion. That was quite good enough for the Justices hearing them.

These bills were tried by juries just as writs were; and as the Justices freed themselves, when managing and directing these trials, from the restraints and shackles of the ordinary procedure in a way which they would never have thought of doing when hearing actions tried under writs, so, I am inclined to think, they treated the jurors trying bills with somewhat more freedom than jurors trying actions by writ, sending them back to reconsider the amount of damages to which a complainant was entitled when they thought that too small a one had been found, and even in a charge of serious crime accepting the verdict of a majority only of the jury, and without thinking of asking for the defendant's consent to such a course. I will give you interesting instances of this from unprinted manuscripts at Lincoln's Inn. At the London Eyre of 1321 John of Hanton complained by bill of a very serious assault made on him by John of Paxton and others. Only Paxton appeared to answer the complaint. Probably the others were not known, as their names are not mentioned. The jury found Paxton guilty and assessed the plaintiff's damages against him at a hundred shillings. A hundred shillings was a reasonably handsome sum in those days. But Hervey of Stanton, the Chief Justice of the Eyre, did not consider it sufficient. He told the jury to consider the serious wound which according to the bill the complainant had received on his head, so large that fourteen pieces of bone had been removed from it.

"Consider, then," he said, "whether you have awarded sufficient damages, even though he had received no other injury." The jury replied that they were finding damages against Paxton alone for his share in the assault, "and we tax the complainant's damages for Paxton's share in his injuries at a hundred shillings. We are not taxing the damages for so much of the wounds as we may suppose was inflicted by others." "That won't do," Stanton told them: "the action is a single one, and you can't divide it up; and therefore even if Paxton struck but one blow you will assess the damages of the whole assault." Then the jury thought the matter over again and assessed the damages at twenty marks, that is £13. 6s. 8d. And the Court ordered that these damages should be paid by Paxton and that he should go to prison; to stay there, I suppose, till he paid them.

At the Northamptonshire Eyre of 4 Edward III a certain bill for assault was tried. The jury retired to consider their verdict, and when they came back they said that they could not agree. Chief Justice Herle asked how they were divided, and was told that eleven were in favour of a verdict of not guilty, while the twelfth man wanted to find the opposite. Herle then questioned the dissenting juror, and asked him why he would not agree with the others. "Sir," he answered, "I myself saw the plaintiff's wound." "Yes," returned Herle, "but did you see the defendant inflict it?" "No, Sir, but I have heard say that he did." "But you did not see the defendant actually inflict the wound and you cannot know that he did inflict it except by seeing him inflict it"; and then the Chief Justice told the jury to deliver their verdict, and they said that the defendant was not guilty. Herle then turned again to the dissentient. "Do you

still refuse to agree with your companions?" "Sir, I do."
Then the Chief Justice accepted the verdict of the eleven
and sent the dissenting twelfth to prison. These remarks
by the Chief Justice suggest criticisms to a modern
lawyer which I am afraid I have not time now to make.

One thing further I must say about these Bills in Eyre
before I pass on to something else. Notes are endorsed
on the backs of most of them of what came of the
complaints which they set out, for which they prayed a
remedy; and we gather from these endorsements that a
surprisingly large number of these bills were either
dropped altogether, or, if prosecuted to a verdict, resulted
in a verdict in favour of the defendant. No doubt the
length of time, often several years, which elapsed between
the commission of the alleged wrong and the coming of
the Eyre, frequently made it impossible to bring anything
like convincing evidence before the Court, and this fact
would account for the failure of many complainants to
prove their alleged facts. But there are the many, very
many, cases where no attempt was made to go on with
the bill. It was sent to the Justices, but the complainant
never prosecuted his complaint. There must have been
some reason for this very frequent failure even to
attempt to substantiate stories of outrage and wrong of
which the most detailed accounts were given, of facts
which must have been within the knowledge of many
people. What was it? One can only guess. But, having
learned what I have learned of the lawless oppression of
the poor and weak in these mediaeval times by their
stronger and richer neighbours and of the corruption of
officials, I am inclined to ask myself whether it is not
at least as likely that these poor folk who made their
detailed complaints of wrong and outrage and then

flinched from prosecuting them to an issue, or, if abiding an issue, not only gained naught by them, but were often fined for not having proved their story, were in the main speaking the truth, as that there was no pressure brought to bear on them to let their complaints drop, no threat of the consequences which would follow perseverance in them; no corrupt election of jurors, no corruption or intimidation of jurors when chosen. I do not myself see my way to believe that the bulk of these complaints which came to naught were mere wicked romances. I cannot see the purpose of them if they were. What we call "blackmailing" could not have been that purpose, for no man minded his reputation over much in those days, and a threat to sue him for damages for any such trespass or outrage as these bills disclose would have affected him not at all. If these complaints had not, as a whole, some real basis of truth in them and were not honest attempts to obtain some compensation for real wrongs really suffered, I do not understand why anyone should have been at the trouble of making and presenting them. This procedure by bill might have been an enormous boon to the people, but its possible benefit was greatly multiplied by the long lapse of time which often necessarily intervened between the commission of the wrong and the coming of the Eyre with the consequent difficulty in procuring evidence, and by other causes of which one can at present assert nothing certainly, but can only hazard a guess. One last word, not altogether an uninteresting one, about these bills. I called them Bills in Eyre when first I had occasion to write about them, for I was obliged to call them by some name. I was quite conscious, however, that more probably than not they were known to the lawyers of the time by some other name. Further study of Year Books of Eyres has disclosed the fact that this was actually the name by which mediaeval lawyers did know them and speak of them.

There are a few minor matters of which I must speak in the short time which remains to me. You will have gathered from what I have already told you that the Justices of the Eyre had to get through an enormous mass of work of one kind and another. Besides all the ordinary assizes and actions which they had to try, there were the interminable presentments in the Crown Pleas, the writs of *quo warranto*, the Gaol Delivery and the Bills, and some other miscellaneous business. If all the Justices had sat together in one single court all this work could not have been got through in any reasonable time. The Kent Eyre of 1313 lasted at least a full year. It seems probable that there were usually three courts sitting. A Year Book of a Northamptonshire Eyre tells us that the Sheriff was bidden to engage three clerks; one to carry out the commands of the Justices hearing Common Pleas, another to be in attendance upon the Justices hearing Rolls, and the third to be in attendance upon the Justices hearing the Pleas of the Crown. This seems to suggest that three separate courts were sitting contemporaneously. Then there was the Gaol Delivery. I cannot say whether a fourth court was sitting separately for that purpose, or whether the prisoners had to wait till the Justices had cleared off some other section of their work. The Year Books tell us nothing about the particular times at which particular kinds of business were taken. They mix up all sorts of things together, and it is exceedingly difficult, I may say impossible, to draw out from them anything like a clear scheme of what happened from day to day and where and before whom it happened.

There are many details of mediaeval procedure which would have much interest and value for us to-day which were matters of such common knowledge to the men of the time that they did not think it worth while formally stating them. Perhaps the information is latent somewhere and further research and study may possibly discover it.

The Justices of the Eyre were out on a great money-making expedition for the King's benefit. How did the King treat them? What financial provision did he make for them? I cannot tell you very much about this, because I do not know very much; but I can tell you something from which you may very reasonably draw further inferences. Let us take the experiences of Hervey of Stanton who presided over the Kent Eyre of 1313. He was a justice of the Common Bench. The *Liberate* Rolls are the only source of information as to the payments made to the Justices of which I have any knowledge. They are for the most part unprinted. In them are enrolled the King's warrants to his Treasurer to pay out certain sums of money. From them we gather that at the time of this Eyre of Kent Stanton's salary as a puisne justice of the Common Bench was forty marks, that is, £26. 13s. 4d. This was all very well in theory, but the trouble was that there was not the least certainty that it would be paid. When Stanton, towards the end of June 1313, went to Canterbury to preside over the Eyre his salary was more than four years in arrears. Nor was this all. During four years of Edward I's reign Stanton had been, previously to his appointment as a Justice of the Common Bench, employed as a Justice to take assizes in the country at a salary of twenty marks a year. All this was still owing to him when he went to Canterbury in the sixth year of Edward II. Little wonder, then, if Stanton, sent down into Kent to preside over a General Eyre, a position which must have made the possession of some ready money almost absolutely necessary, found himself—and such examination of the *Liberate* Rolls as I have made does not lead me to suppose that his fellow Justices of the Eyre were in better plight—compelled to make some urgent representation to the King as to his own and his fellow Justices' needs. I presume that some special application was made to the King, for the King just at this time takes an unusual course, which he would probably have taken only to satisfy some urgent demand. There is no money, apparently, in the Treasury with which to pay his Justices in Kent, and so he sends an order to the Sheriff to draw upon the fines and amercements which the Justices have been levying and the Sheriff has been receiving on the King's account for that purpose. Stanton is to have 60 marks, William of Ormsby 50 marks, and the other Justices 40 marks apiece for their expenses in the Eyre. And with this sop of 60 marks Hervey of Stanton has to get on as best he can until he can extract from the Treasury towards the end of June 1315, a couple of years later, some of the long standing arrears of his salary. If it were at all the general usage for the Justices of the Eyre to be dependent for their living expenses on the fines and amercements they inflicted we can all the better understand the old reporter's comparison of them with lions ready to spring on their prey. But as a matter of fact, I may tell you here incidentally, the King's Justices had sources of income upon which to rely other than those official salaries which they might or might not receive. The accounts of the Knights Hospitallers in England for the

year 1338 happen to have survived, and they have some
rather interesting revelations to make. Geoffrey the
Scrope, who was then Chief Justice of the King's Bench,
had a lease for life from the Knights of a house at
Huntingdon of the yearly value of ten marks and he was
released from the obligation of paying any rent for it.
He had another house at Penhall, together with meadows
and pastures and other land on the same easy terms.
And besides all this he had a pension of forty shillings a
year from the Knights as Chief Justice of the King's
Bench, "in which court all pleas of trespasses and felony
and conspiracy are pleaded," words which seem to con-
stitute a fairly frank confession of the reason which lay
at the back of the Knights' minds when they made all
this comfortable provision for the Chief Justice. Richard
Willoughby, a Justice of the same court, had a pension
of five marks. The whole of the Justices of the Common
Bench, the Court, to quote the note in the account book,
in which pleas of land and tenements were heard and
determined, were receiving pensions from the Knights.
Chief Justice Herle took forty pounds a year, which was
exactly the amount of his official salary as Chief Justice,
and I daresay that the Knights would take care in their
own interests to be more punctual paymasters than the
King. The puisne Justices took smaller amounts. The
Barons of the Exchequer were also all subsidized, and the
minor officials of the several courts also. And perhaps
it is not altogether unreasonable to suppose that the
Justices were drawing other like pensions from other like
sources. But I do not forget, and I will ask you not to
forget the financial difficulties into which they were driven
by the King's neglect to pay them the salaries to which
they were entitled. The fact remains plain that they were

often left, more often than not, without any salary at all for year after year, and whether they, or even their executors, were ever able to recover the arrears owing to them is very doubtful. And Judges, like other people had to live. We need not, therefore, think too hardly of them because, driven by necessity, they allowed themselves to accept what seemed the only income on which they could certainly count.

In reading the Year Books of the Eyres we find the Justices often impressing upon us the fact that one of the reasons why the Eyre was established was that men might get speedy and full justice. And to be as good as their word, and to avoid delays, the Justices drew upon their royal powers; and if it were objected that they were doing things which the Justices of the Bench had no power to do, they quietly retorted: "You are talking nonsense; we can do many things which they cannot do," and they did them. I do not know how the rather strange theory that the whole session of the Eyre, no matter how long it might be, constituted but a single day arose, but that undoubtedly was the working theory. It is often specifically stated. Perhaps the theory that the Eyre was established for the speedy rendering of justice was put forth first, and then to give some sort of support to that theory this second theory was evolved, for if it could be said that all the work a long Eyre got through was done in a single day, then, doubtless, the Eyre was much the speediest machine for the administration of justice that has ever been invented. This theory that the Eyre lasted only a single day had one rather important consequence, which must have often worked to the advantage of many people to whom it was, perhaps, not very desirable to extend advantages. I mentioned in my first lecture that the ceremony of outlawry could be performed only at a session of the county court. I mentioned also that the Eyre was in itself the full county court. Before a man could be outlawed he had to be what was called "exacted," that is, formally summoned to surrender himself to the law, at five consecutive county courts. At the last of these five, if he did not appear, he was formally outlawed. As the county courts were held every month the process of outlawry normally took four months. If an Eyre were in session the fugitive from justice got a much longer period of grace, which might, it would seem, run to nearer four years than four months. "If a man," says one of our old manuscripts, "be exacted in Eyre, though the Eyre last two years or three, the whole of the Eyre shall be reckoned as only one county court."

Lastly, when did the Eyres cease and why? Probably their unpopularity had no little to do with hastening their end, but the effective reason which the old authorities give is the increased powers granted by several Acts of Parliament to the Justices of Assizes and other commissions, as a result of which the Eyres little by little vanished away. There do not seem to have been any after 10 Edward III (1336); and, so far as I know, there is no record that any one mourned their decease.

And now my story must perforce end. I have told my tale as well and as fully as I have found myself able to tell it in three short lectures. I have had to leave unsaid very much which I should have liked to say, to omit many a detail of fact and description, much by way of explanation and illustration and comment, which it would have been not amiss to say, and not, I think, without interest for you to hear. But it could not be. The subject is indeed too big a one to be dealt with adequately within the limitations of my time. But yet I hope that I have been able to say enough, that I have said enough, in one way and another, to leave you with some real, though very incomplete, picture of a mediaeval General Eyre; to enable you to understand in perhaps some livelier and fuller way than you had realized before something of what an Eyre was, something of what it did, and of what it meant for the people of the time.

INDEX

Printed in the United States
By Bookmasters